ArT RANDOM

David Mach

Edited by Marco Livingstone

KYOTO SHOIN

First published in Japan 1990 by KYOTO SHOIN INTERNATIONAL Co., Ltd.
Sanjo agaru, Horikawa, Nakagyo-ku, Kyoto, Japan. TEL[075]841-9123
Second : 1991

Editorial director : Kyoichi Tsuzuki
Art director : Ichiro Miyagawa

© Copyright 1990 : David Mach
Text copyright 1990 : Marco Livingstone

All works are reproduced by courtesy of Galerie Michael Werner,
Köln and Galerie Claude Bernard, Paris.

ISBN4-7636-8576-7 C0371 P1980E

Printed and bound in Kyoto by SHASHIN KAGAKU Co., Ltd.

Translation : Fia, Inc.

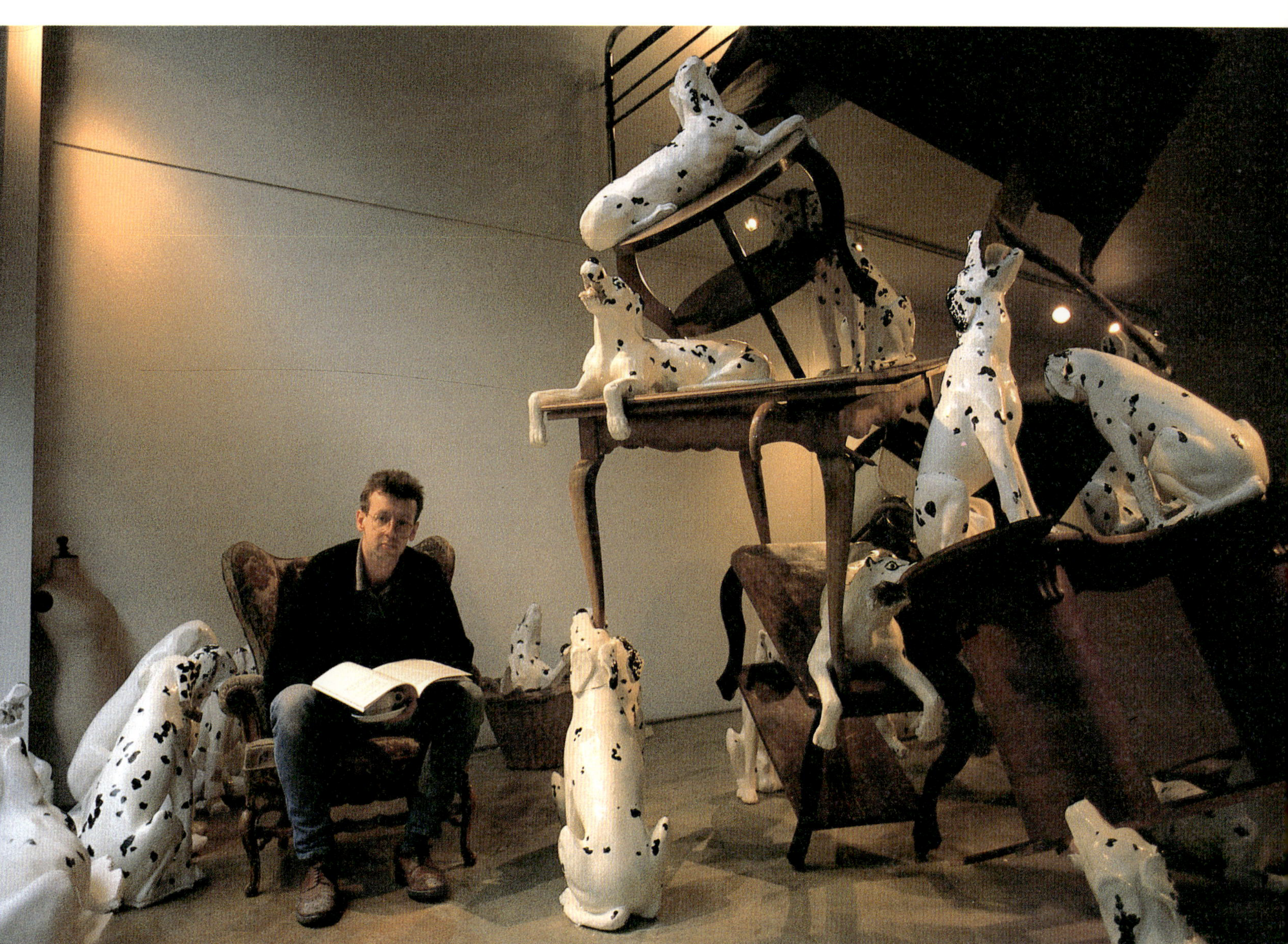

TAMED, TRAINED AND FRAMED / Galerie Maurice Kietelman, Brussels / Photographer - Arthur Foster

DAVID MACH

David Mach was born on 18 March 1956 at Methil, Fife, Scotland, and studied at the Duncan of Jordanstone College of Art in Dundee (1974-9) and at the Royal College of Art in London (1979-82). He began developing his highly original conception of temporary public sculptures on a massive scale while still a student in Scotland in works made from discarded junk and from natural elements, as in the case of a suspended 'carpet' approximately 15 metres long woven from fallen leaves gathered together in Camperdown Park in Dundee. It was after his arrival in London, however, that he made his first pieces from massive quantities of identical mass-produced objects, beginning with a life-size replica of a Rolls-Royce constructed from 15000 books. Keen to relate his activity as an artist to the experiences of the population at large - and specifically to the factory jobs that he had taken over the years to support himself as a student - Mach realized at once the potential of books, magazines, telephone directories, bottles, car tyres, and other materials from industry transformed into recognizable images through simple procedures such as layering and stacking.

While other British sculptors working in the 1980s, such as Tony Cragg and Bill Woodrow, commented on the built-in obsolescence of machine-made consumer items, Mach has made a point of using large quantities of unused objects made available to him because they were surplus to requirements. Every one of his sculptures thus impli-citly raises the issues of the overproduction and overconsumption of western society, drawing attention to our wastefulness and to the excessive importance accorded to material possessions. While others of his generation have made reference to such concerns, only Mach has consistently adhered to the belief that to counter this materialism his own sculptures should have only a temporary existence. His work suggests that there are enough objects in the world already, and that to add to them would be to collude with the market forces of which he is critical. Although his art by definition escapes treatment as a commodity or investment, it acknowledges its wider dependence on society: in almost every case the materials have to be sponsored either by loan or gift, and the sculptures are generally assembled by a team of friends and assistants in front of the public, who are encouraged to ask questions and to engage in the spirit of the work.

Over the years Mach has evolved various categories, which he has continued to elaborate as his own sculptural language. Many of his early pieces, representing immediately recognizable things such as a submarine, were assembled from thousands of unsold magazines or books; these led in turn not only to ironic reworkings of classical sculptural traditions, as in the case of the monumental columns of Liberté, Egalité, Fraternité (June 1989), but to more elaborate narratives. In Fuel for the Fire (August 1986), Natural Causes (September 1987) and A Million Miles Away (May 1988), for example, real objects seem either to be swept along by a torrent of such material or to spew them out as unwanted things that had outlived their usefulness. A separate category, also developed early in the 1980s, was of rows of glass bottles some of which were filled with coloured dyes to form emblematic images whose outlines become recognizable only when viewed from certain angles: such is the case with several works in which the design of a national flag doubles as the image of a woman lying on her back with her legs outstretched in sexual anticipation. Mach's delight in incongruities of scale, which forms an essential background to the irony of his huge monuments to transience, finds form in works in which huge objects such as real cars, buses and fallen trees appear to be held aloft by tiny dolls, teddy bears and toy figures. In some recent works, such as those using ornamental dogs or inflatable seals, the individual components are themselves images commanding our attention, while in others, such as the chain of tables featured in Wet & Dry (October 1989), the objects, while retaining their original identity, are orchestrated in a more abstract manner. Mach's work, while respectful of certain sculptural traditions, remains fundamentally subversive, recognizing only those rules that will assure for each project the greatest impact and the most memorable experience for its particular audience.

Marco Livingstone

デヴィッド・マック

デヴィッド・マックは1956年3月18日スコットランド、ファイフのメシルに生まれ、ダンディーのジョーダンストン芸術大学ダンカン校(1974-9)及びロンドンの王立芸術大学(1979-82)に学んだ。公共空間を使った巨大な一時的彫刻という極めて独創的なコンセプトを転開しはじめたころ、マックはまだスコットランドの一学生だった。当時の作品はダンディーのキャンパーダウン公園で捨った落ち葉を編合わせた長さ15メートルにおよぶ「カーペット」のように、ゴミや自然物を素材に使用している。しかしながら、1万5000冊の本でできた実物大のロールス・ロイスのレプリカを初めとして、大量生産された一製品を多量に使用した作品を始めたのはロンドンにやってきてからのことである。アーティストとしての活動を一般大衆の体験…とりわけ学生時代の数年間自活のために従事した工場作業…と関連づけることに心を砕いたマックは、本、雑誌、電話帳、瓶、タイヤなどの工業製品が、ただ積み上げるというような単純な手法によってある認識可能なイメージに変貌する、そのような可能性にすぐ気がついたのである。

トニー・クラッグやビル・ウッドローなど1980年代の英国彫刻家たちは、大量生産消費材に備わるはかなさについてさまざまな批評を加えてきたが、マックは供給過剰によって容易に入手できる未使用製品を大量に使うようになった。このようにマックの作品ひとつひとつは、西欧社会の過剰生産と過剰消費の問題を包含し、我々の犯す無駄と無質所有偏重へと目を向けさせる。マックと同年代の彫刻家たちもまたこうした懸念を口にするいっぽうで、マックただひとりが、こうした物質主義に対抗するためには自分の作品は一時的存在でなければならないという信念にこだわってきた。その作品が示唆するのは、この世界では物が十分あること、そのうえに物を増やすことは彼が批判的に見ている市場勢力との共謀を意味する、ということである。彼の作品は、定義上は商品、投資としての扱いは免がれていても、社会からの広範な依存からはのがれられない。つまり、ほとんどどんな場合でも材料は貸与あるいは譲渡に頼らねばならないし、作品は友人や助手の手を借りて、公衆が質問を投げかけたり作品の真髄に触れたりできるようその前面で組み上げられることがほんどだからである。

幾年間にもわたって様々な分野に手を拡げつつ、マックは自信の彫刻言語を練上げてきた。たとえば潜水艦のように、即座に見分けのつくなにかを表現している初期の作品の多くは、数千冊の雑誌や本の売れ残りを組み上げたものであった。これが発展して「自由、平等、友愛」(1989年6月)の記念柱のように、古典的彫刻の伝統を皮肉をこめて再生するようになり、またさらに手の込んだ物語となる。たとえば「火に油」(1986年8月)、「天災」(1987年9月)、「100万マイルの彼方」(1988年5月)では、対象物が素材の波に洗い流されてしまったり、もはや役目を終えた無用の長物の如く吐き出されてしまっているようにもみえる。1980年代初めから進められたもうひとつのジャンルは空瓶を並べ、中の何本かには染料が入っているため、ある角度から見たときだけ象徴的にイメージの輪郭が浮かび上がるというものである。一例としてあげられるのが、国旗の図柄が、性的期待に満ちて足を大開きく広げて仰向けに寝ている女性のイメージと、二重写しになるいくつかの作品である。巨大でしかも一時的なモニュメントというアイロニーの本質的背景を成すスケールの法外さをマックは楽しんでいて、それが本物の車やバス、倒木などの巨大な物体が小さな人形や熊のぬいぐるみやおもちゃに持ち上げられている作品に、かたちとなって現れている。置物の犬やビニールのアザラシなどを使った近作では、構成物そのものが我々の注意を引くイメージになっているいっぽうで、テーブルをつなげた「ウエット＆ドライ」(1989年10月)のように構成物本来のアイデンティティを保ちながらも、より抽象的な姿に組み上げられているものもある。マックの作品は、ある部分彫刻の伝統に忠実でありながらも、根本的に破壊的であって、最大のインパクトと、忘れられない体験とを観る者に与えることをプロジェクトのひとつひとつに保証する、そのような法則のみを受け入れているといえよう。

マルコ・リヴィングストン

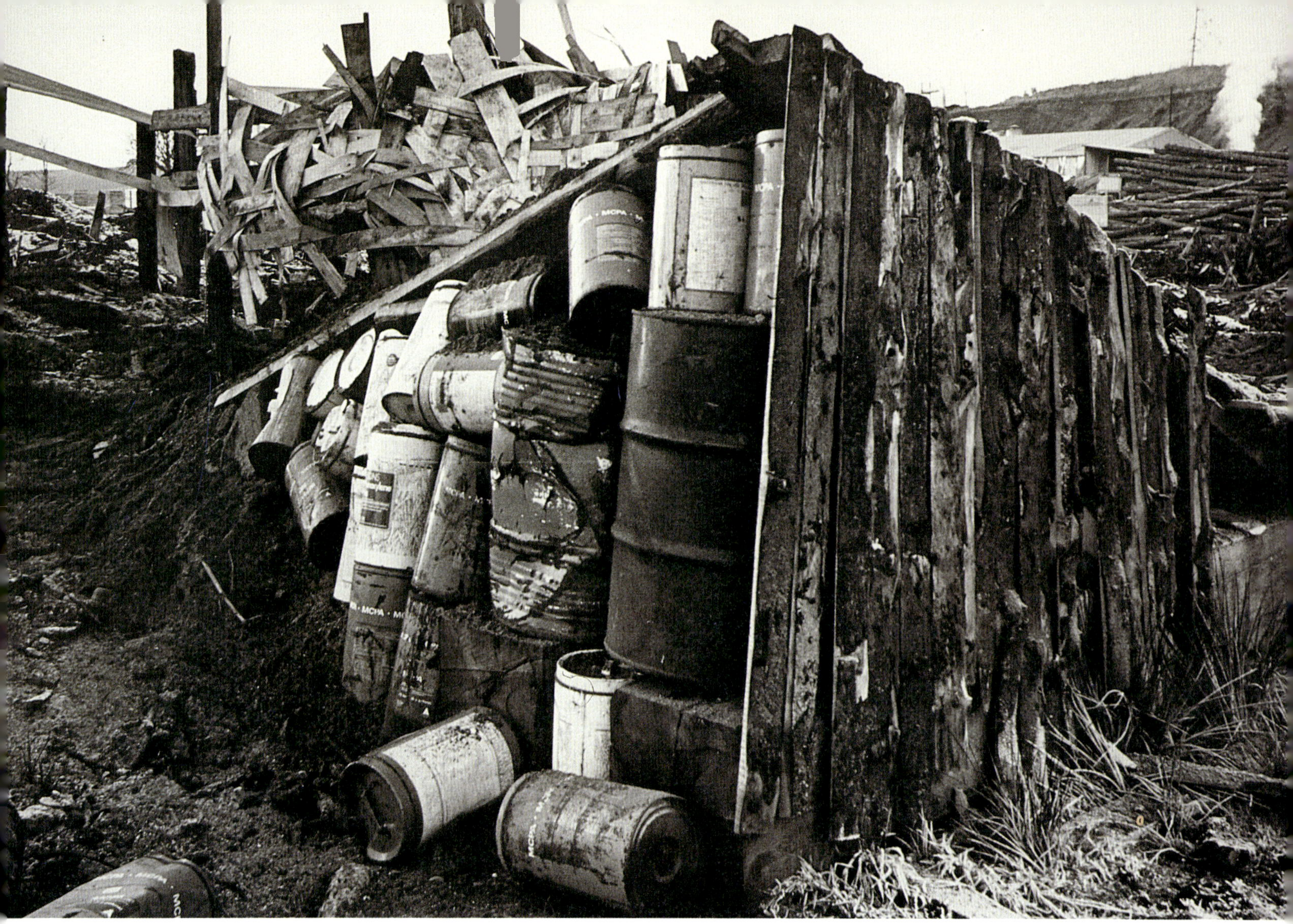

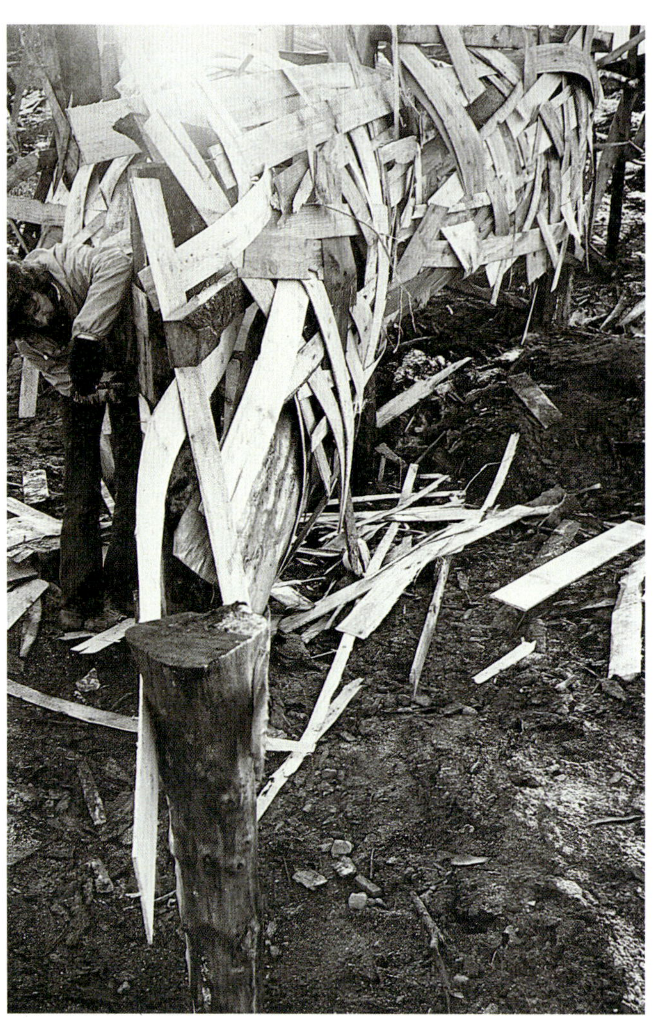

ALYTH SAWMILL / Alyth, Scotland / December 1978 / Photographer - Michael Davey

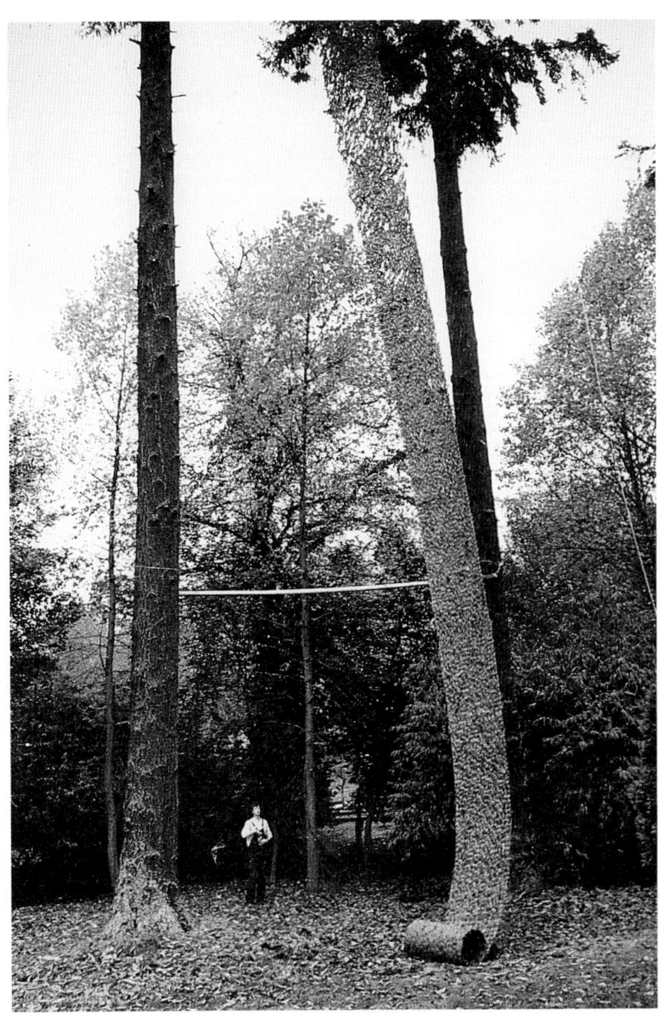

CAMPERDOWN PARK / Dundee, Scotland / October 1979. / Photographer - Michael Davey

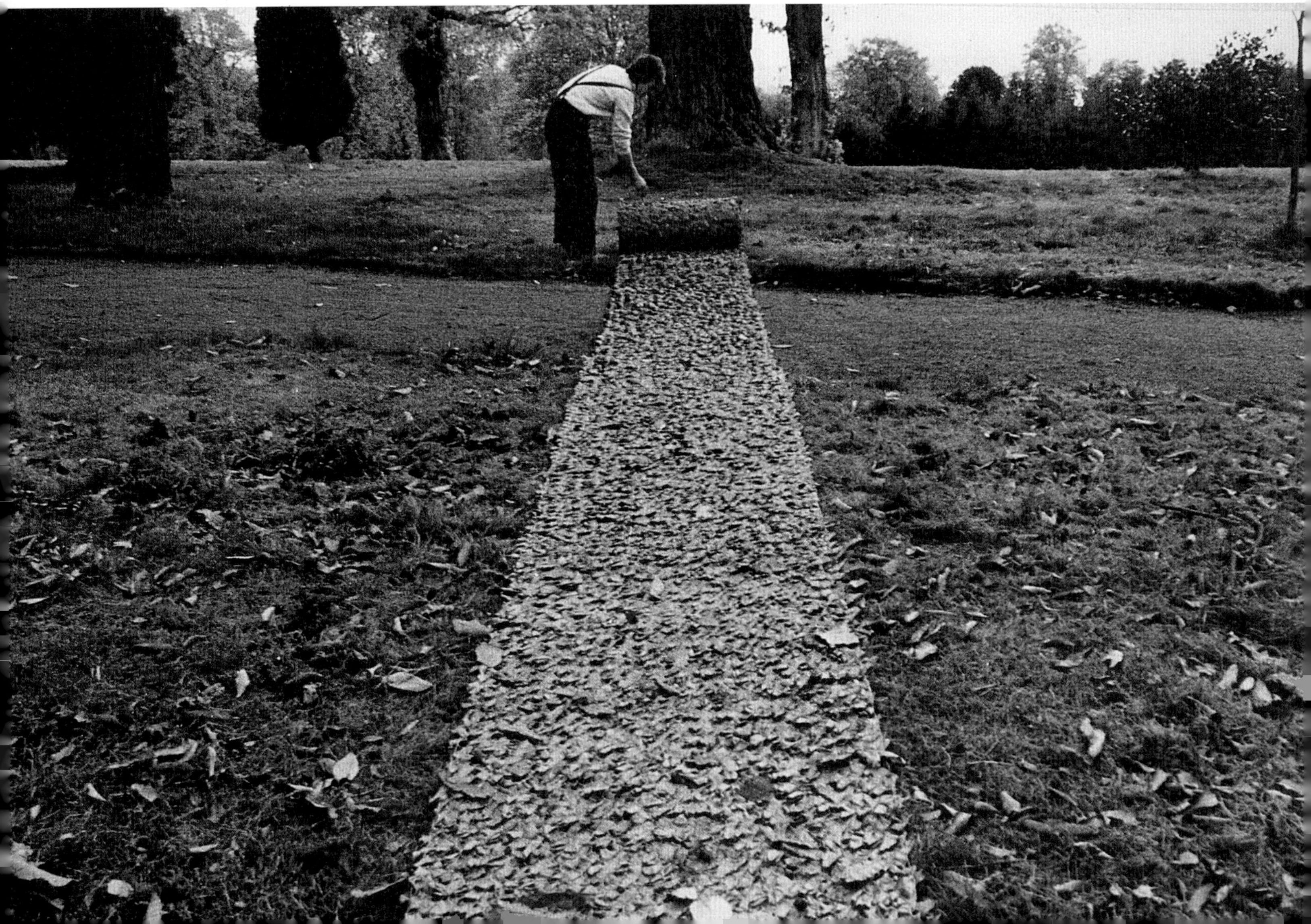

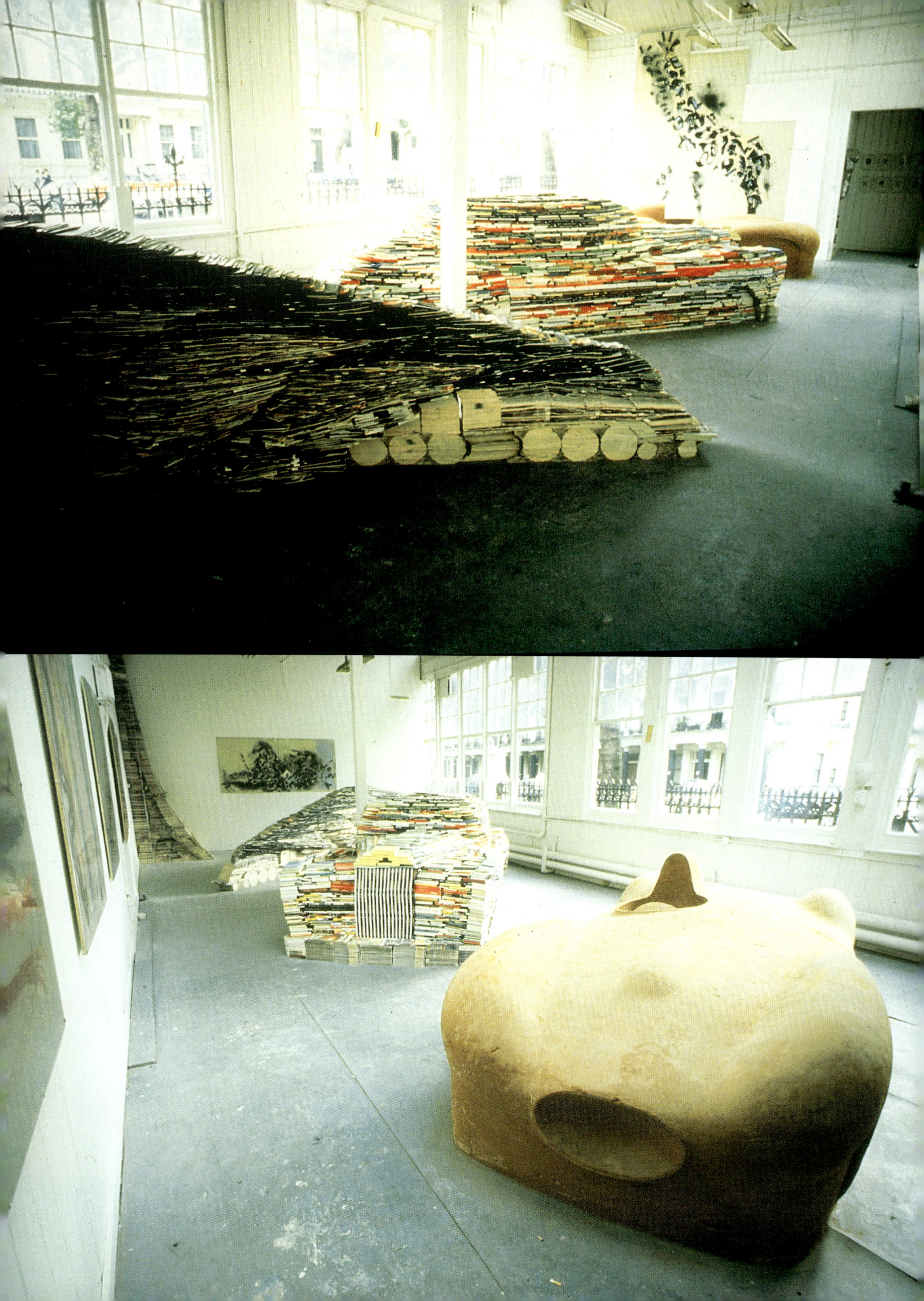

D TYPE JAG / SILVER CLOUD III / RUNNING OUT OF STEAM / LA TOUR EIFFEL / LION + T. SQUARE
Royal College of Art. Degree show / June 1982 / Photographer - Artist

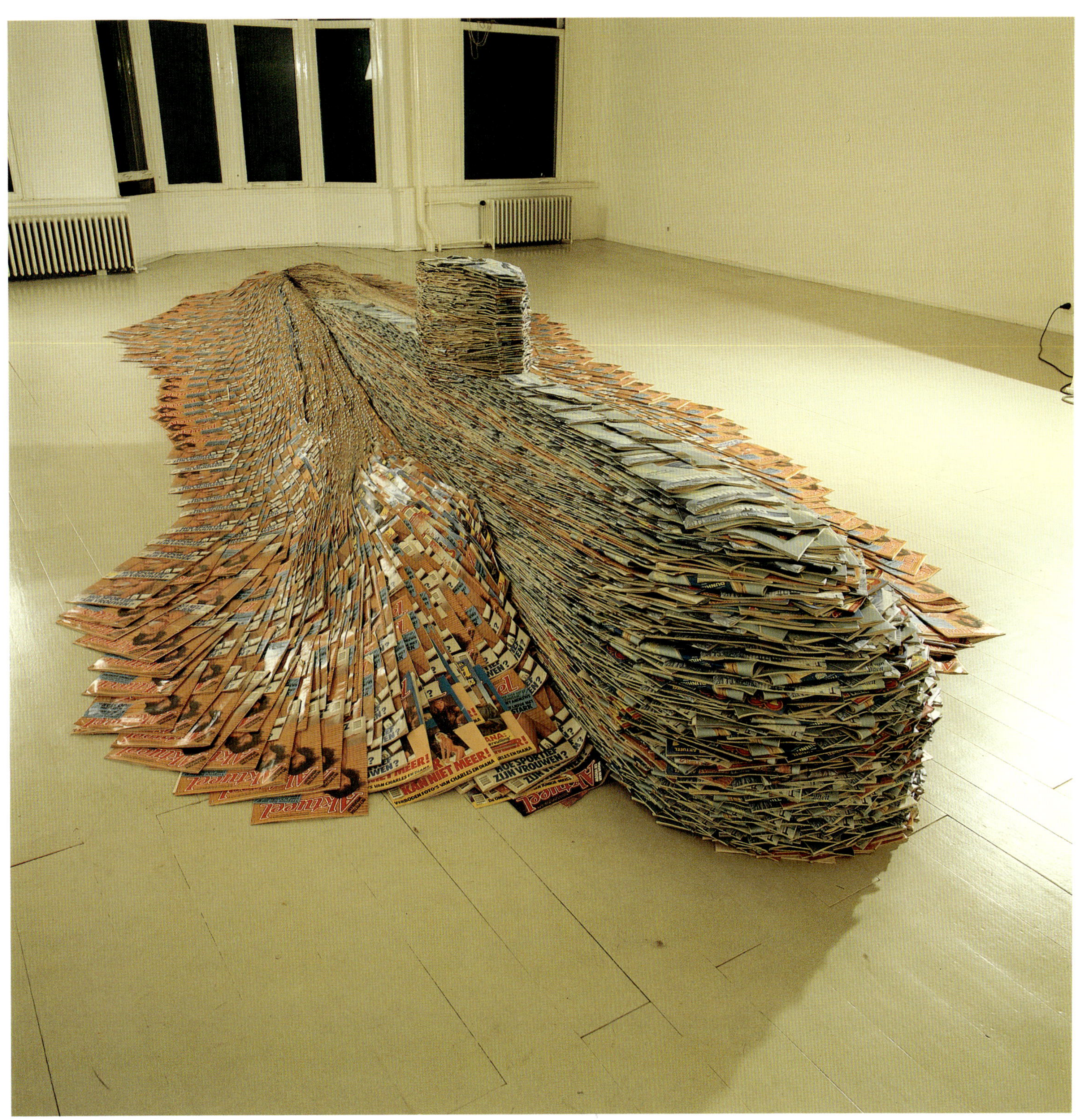

SILENT RUNNING / Galerie t'Venster, Rotterdam / December 1982.

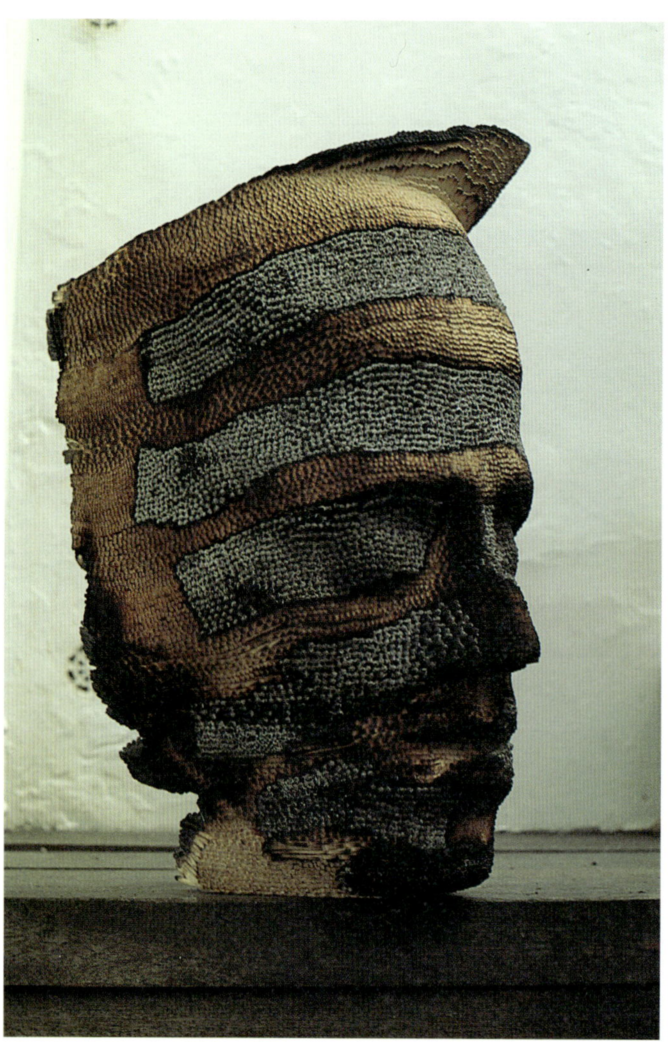

KINSKY HEAD / Collection - Tom Bendhem. / December 1982

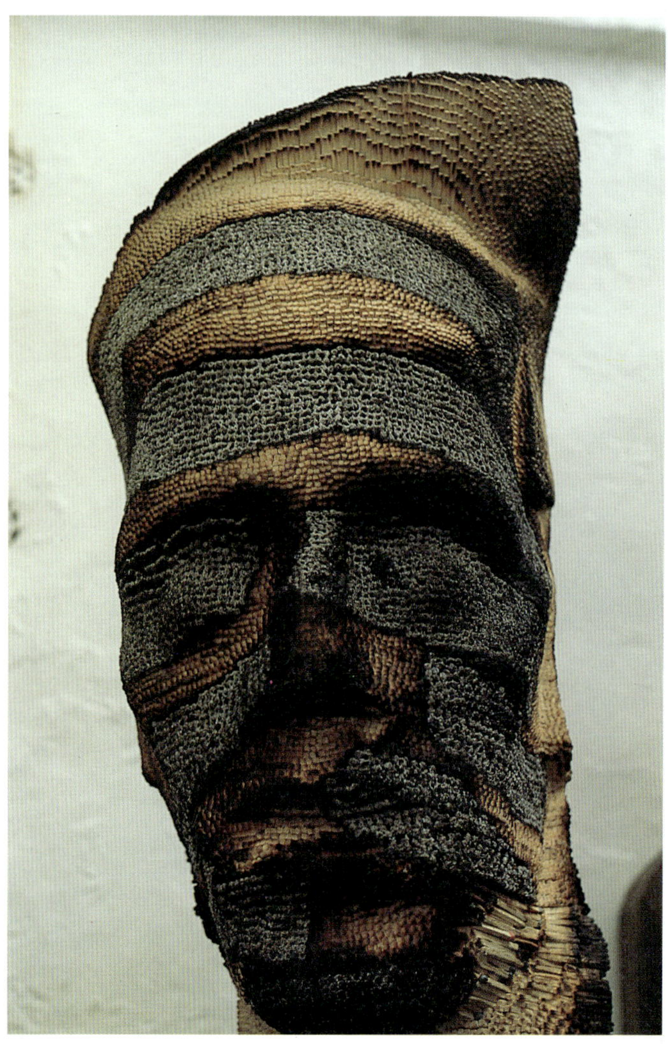

Opposite : POLARIS / British Sculpture '83 / Hayward Gallery, London. / August 1983

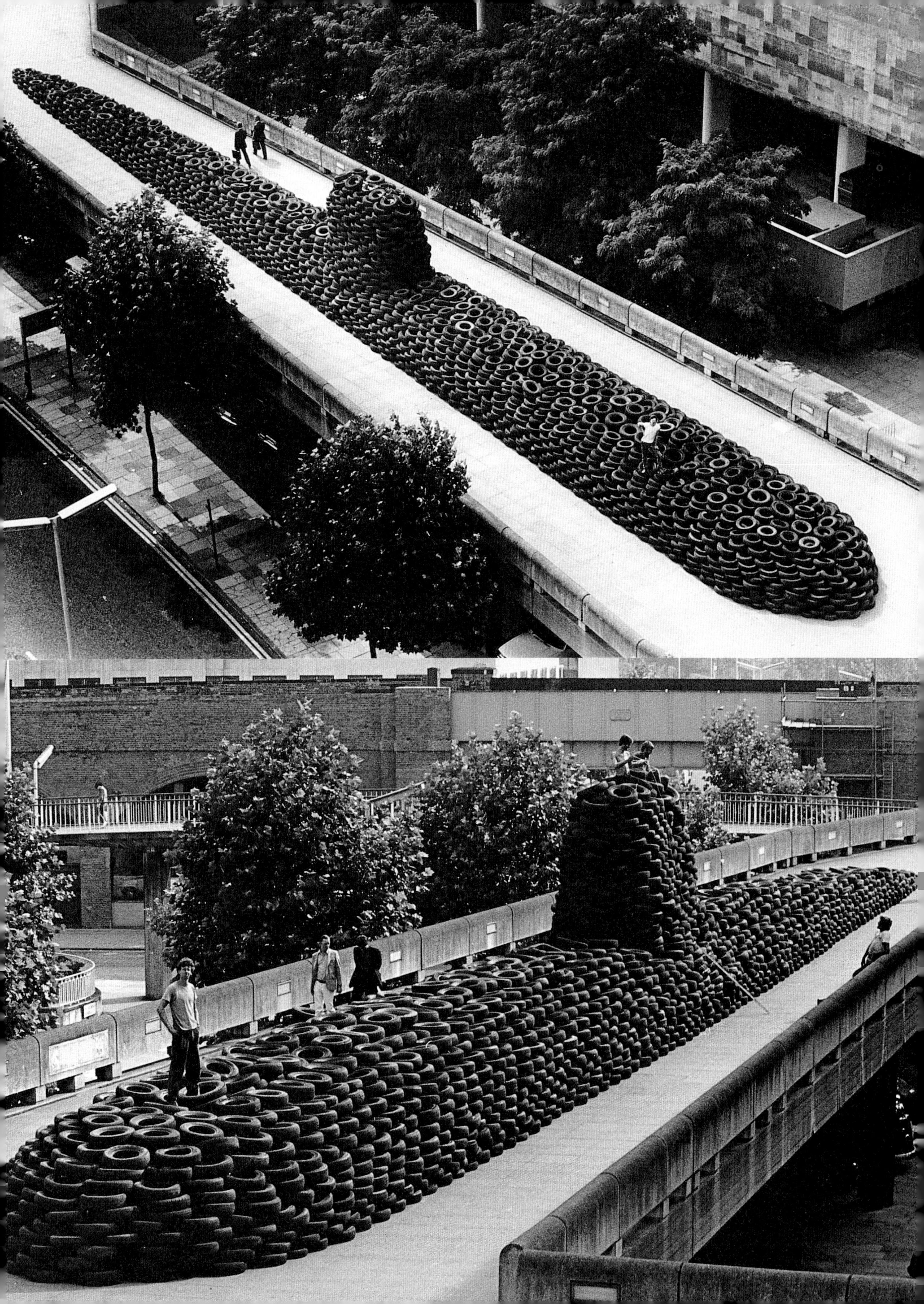

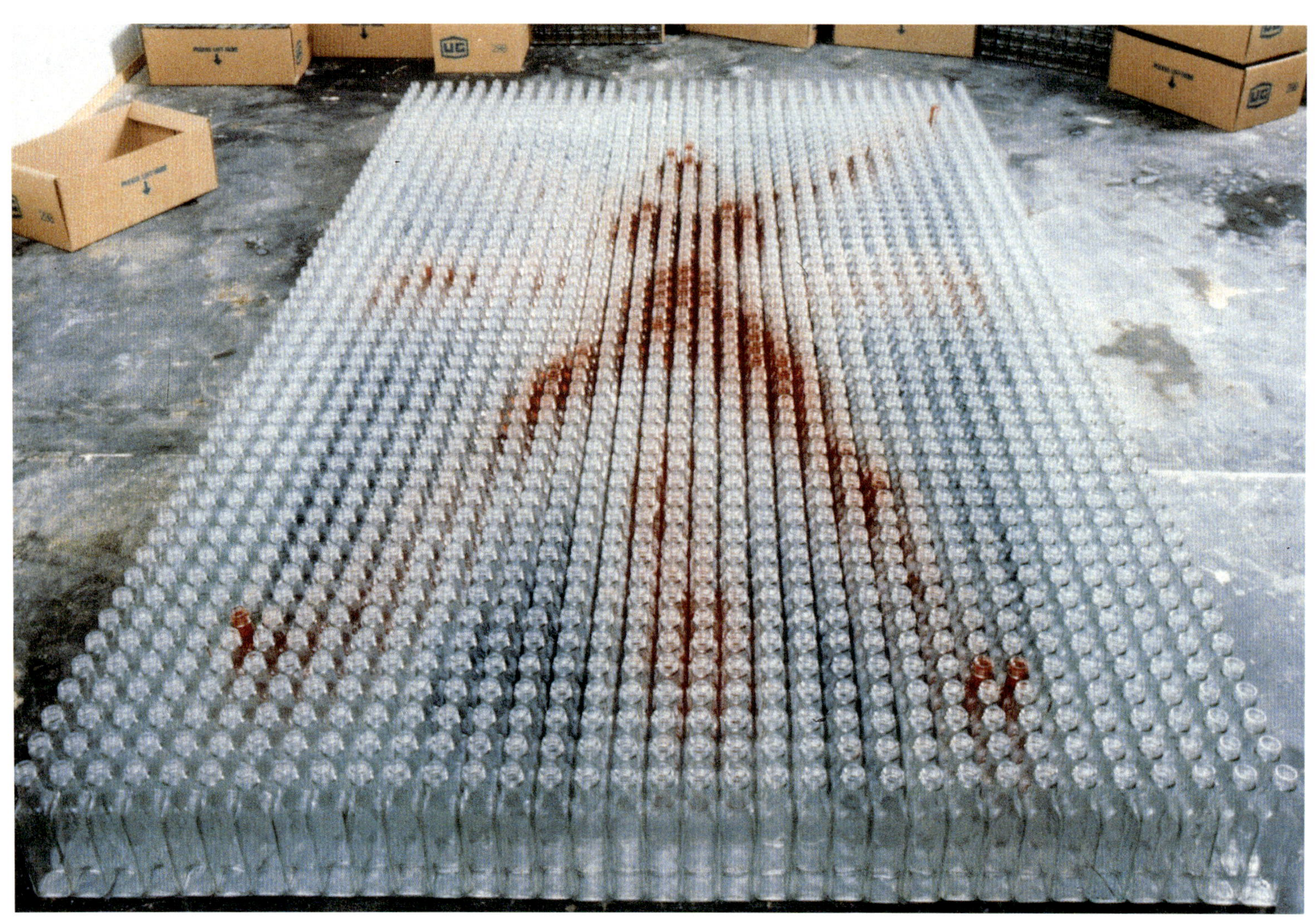

THINKING OF ENGLAND / Arts Review '83 / London Weekend Television / December 1983 / Collection - Tate Gallery, Liverpool.

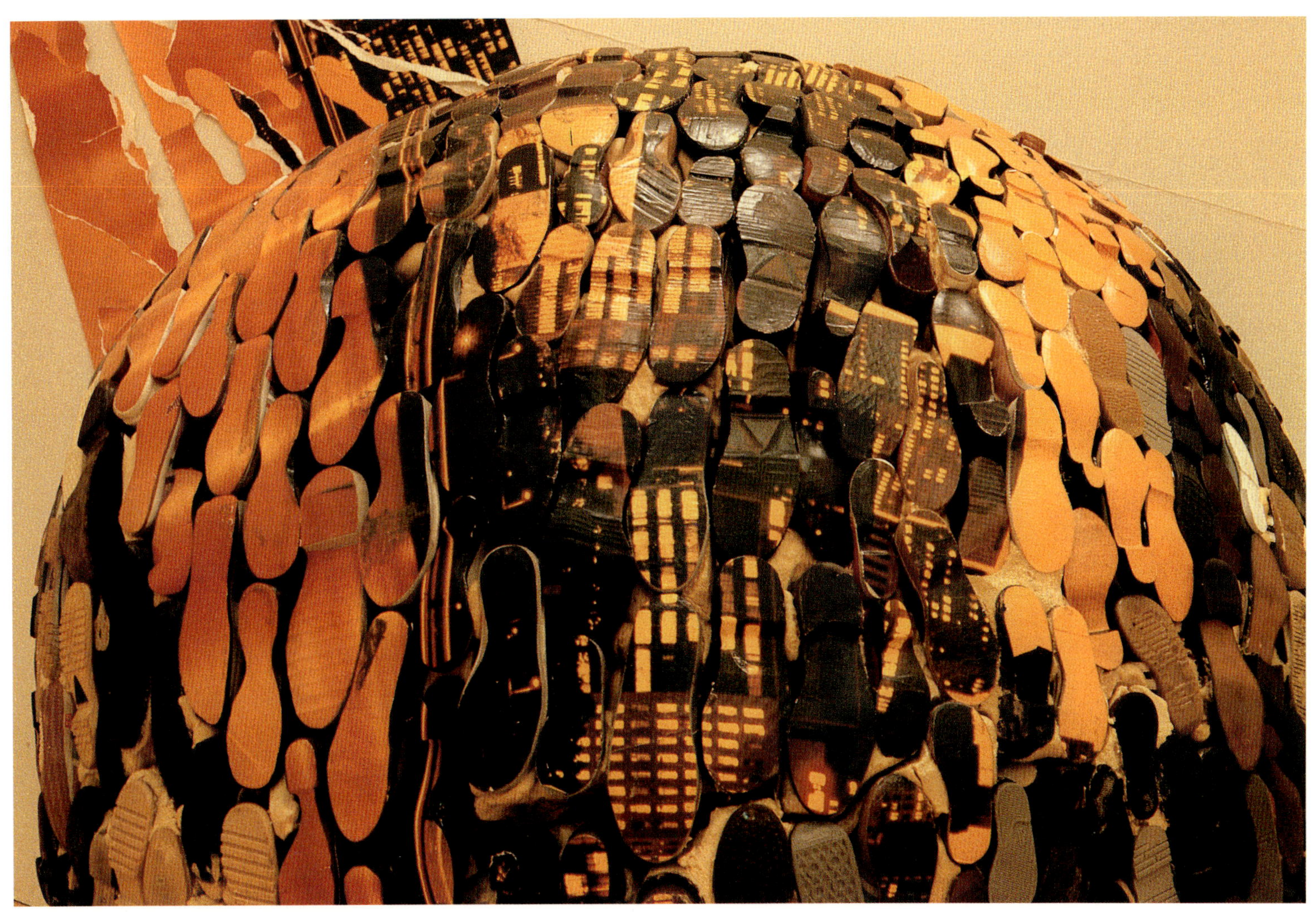

FOXTROT / TOWARDS A LANDSCAPE / Museum of Modern Art, Oxford / February 1985

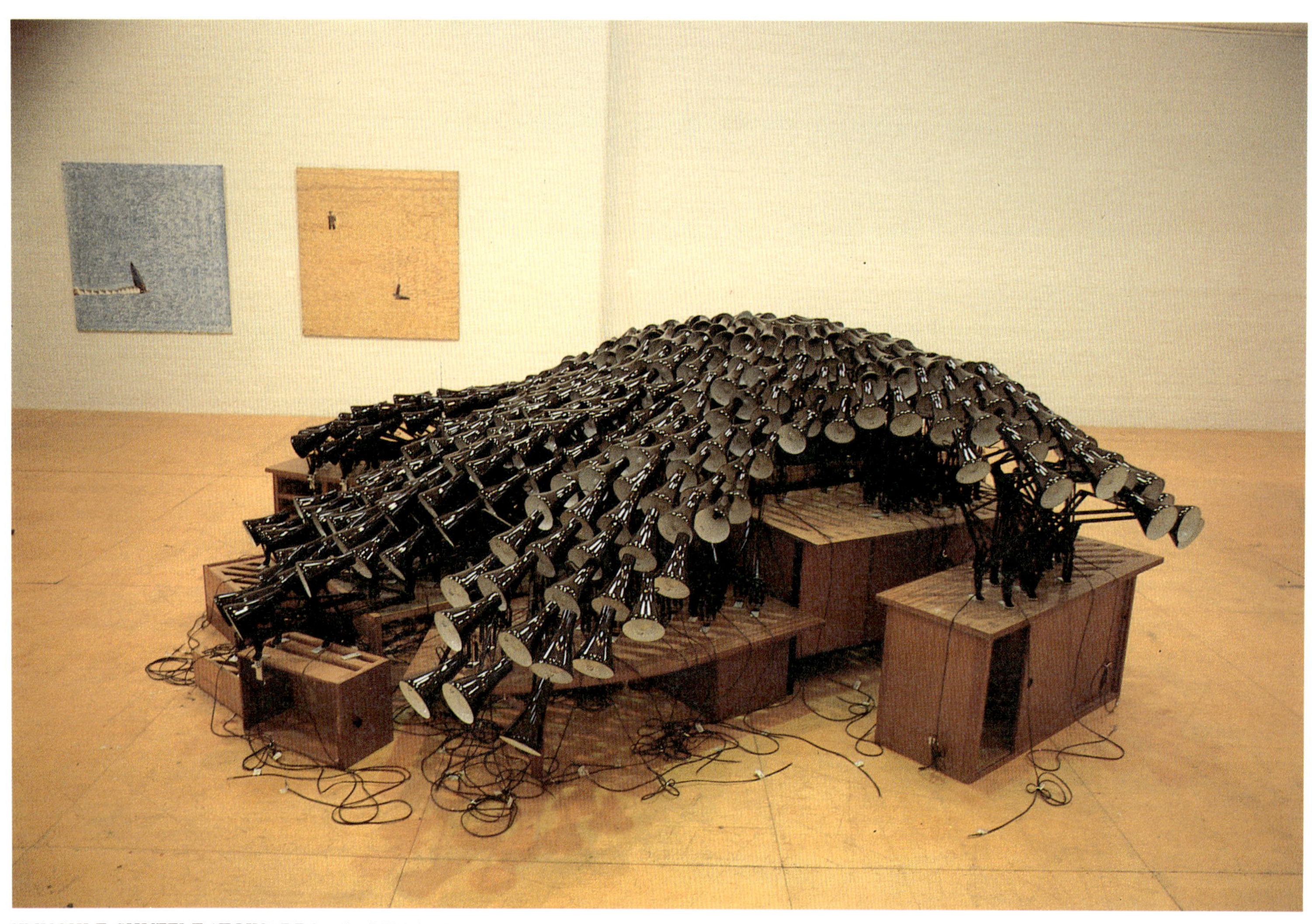

KNUCKLE-SHUFFLE / TOWARDS A LANDSCAPE / Museum of Modern Art, Oxford / February 1985

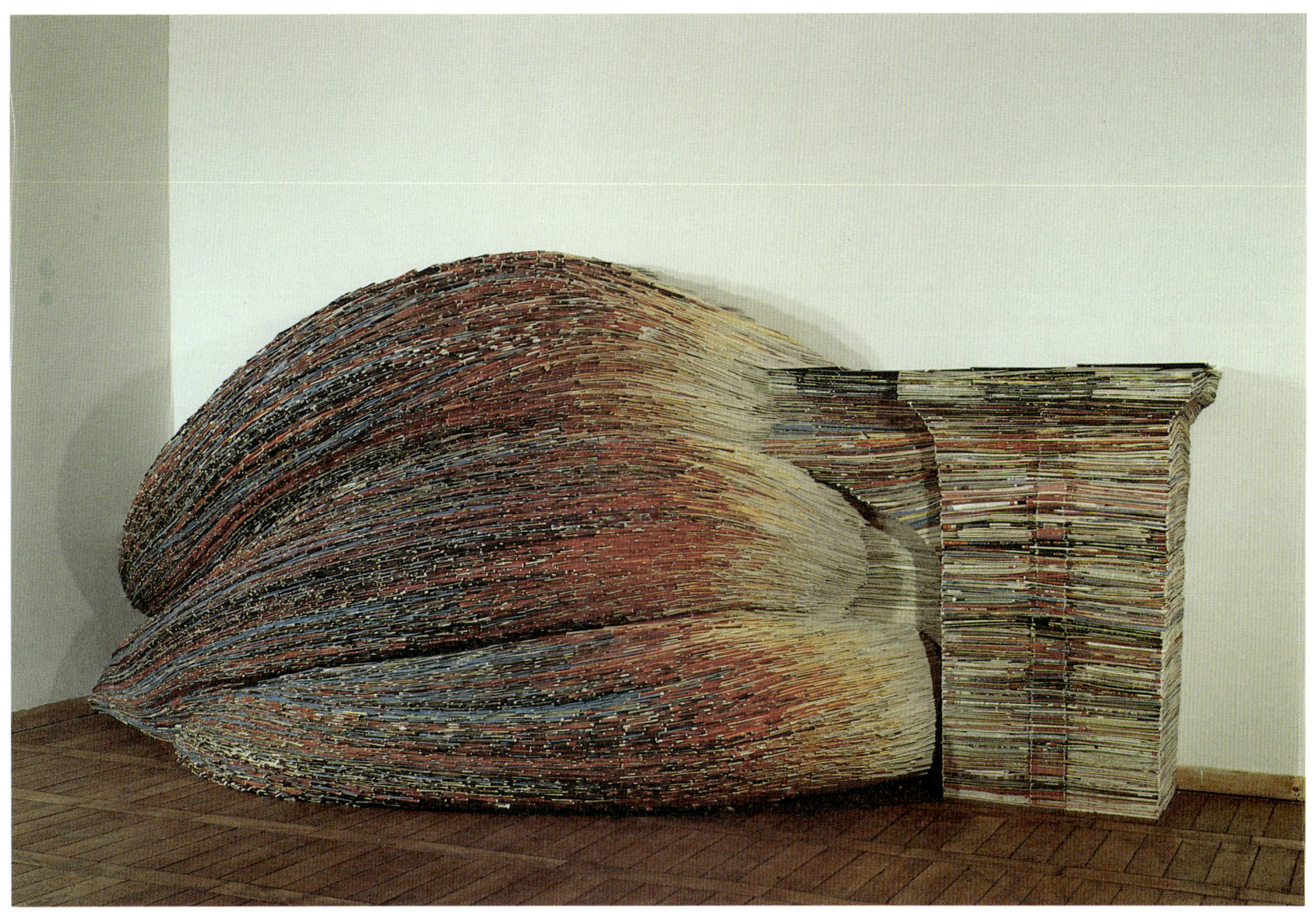

UNTITLED / Galerie Foksal, Warsaw / October 1985

Following Page : PARTHENON / AUTOMOBIENNALE / Middelheim Museum, Antwerp / June 1985
P18-19 : HACKNEY CAB / The Interim Art Wall, Ceiling, Floorshow with Artangel Roadshow, London / June 1985

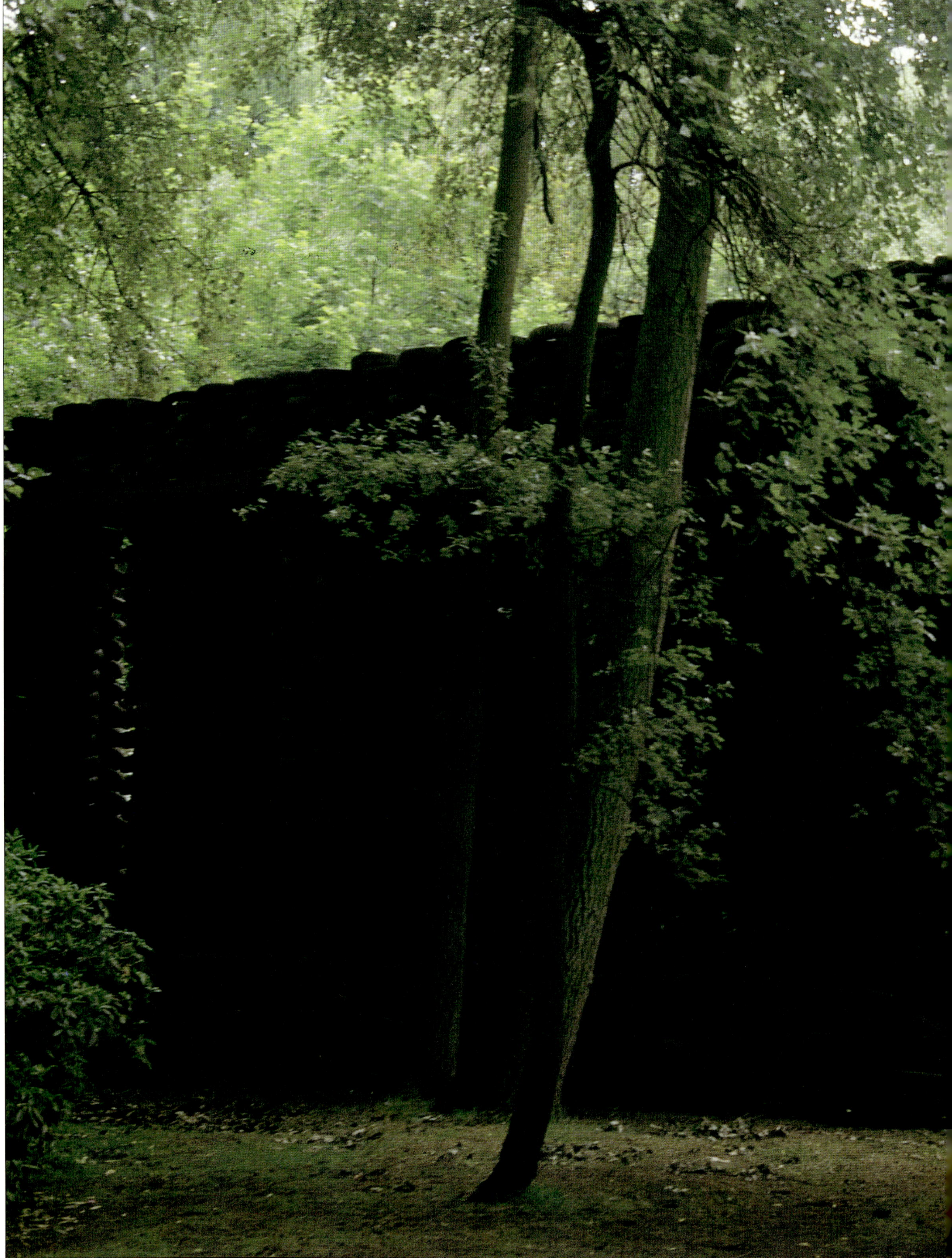

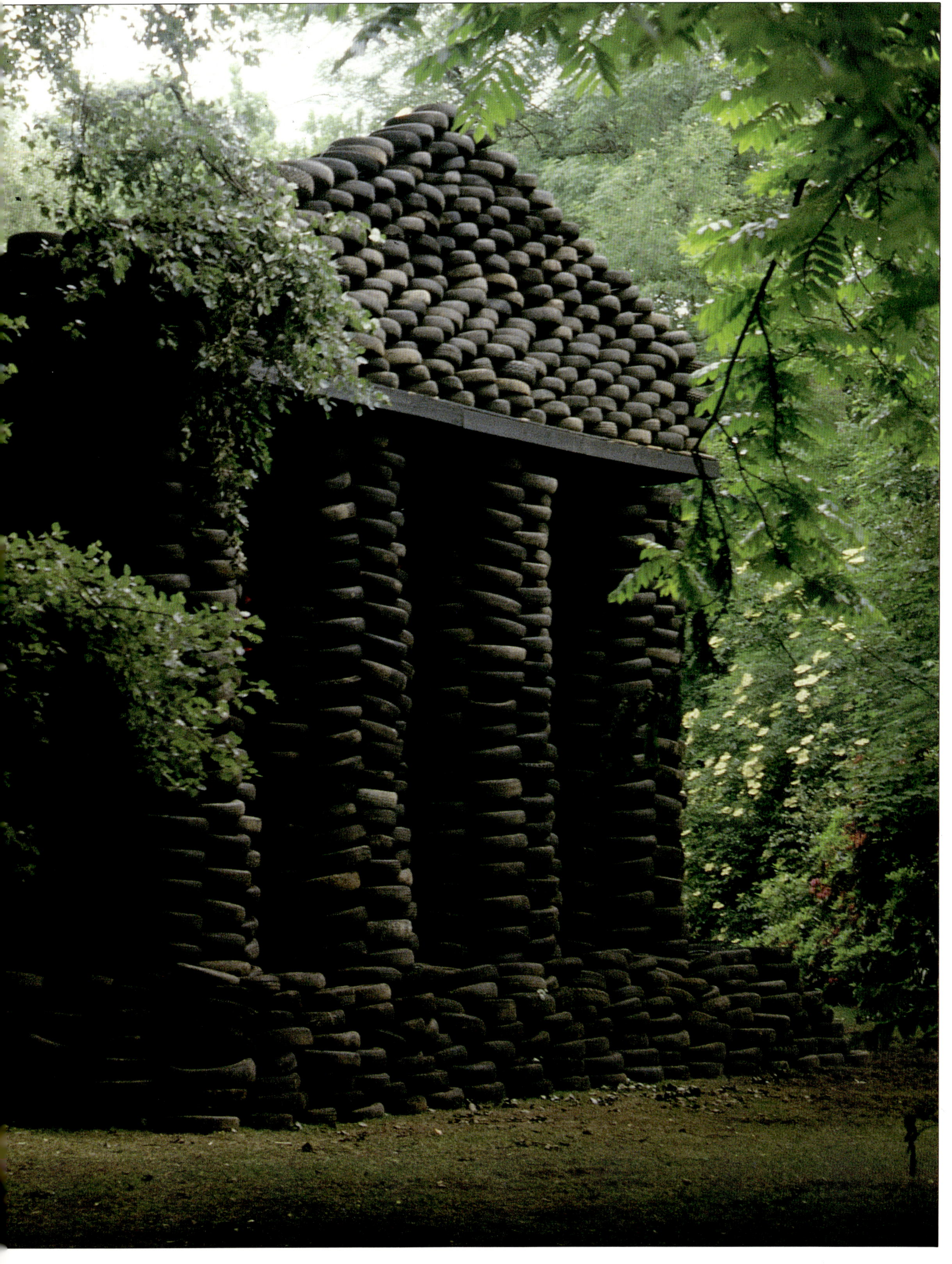

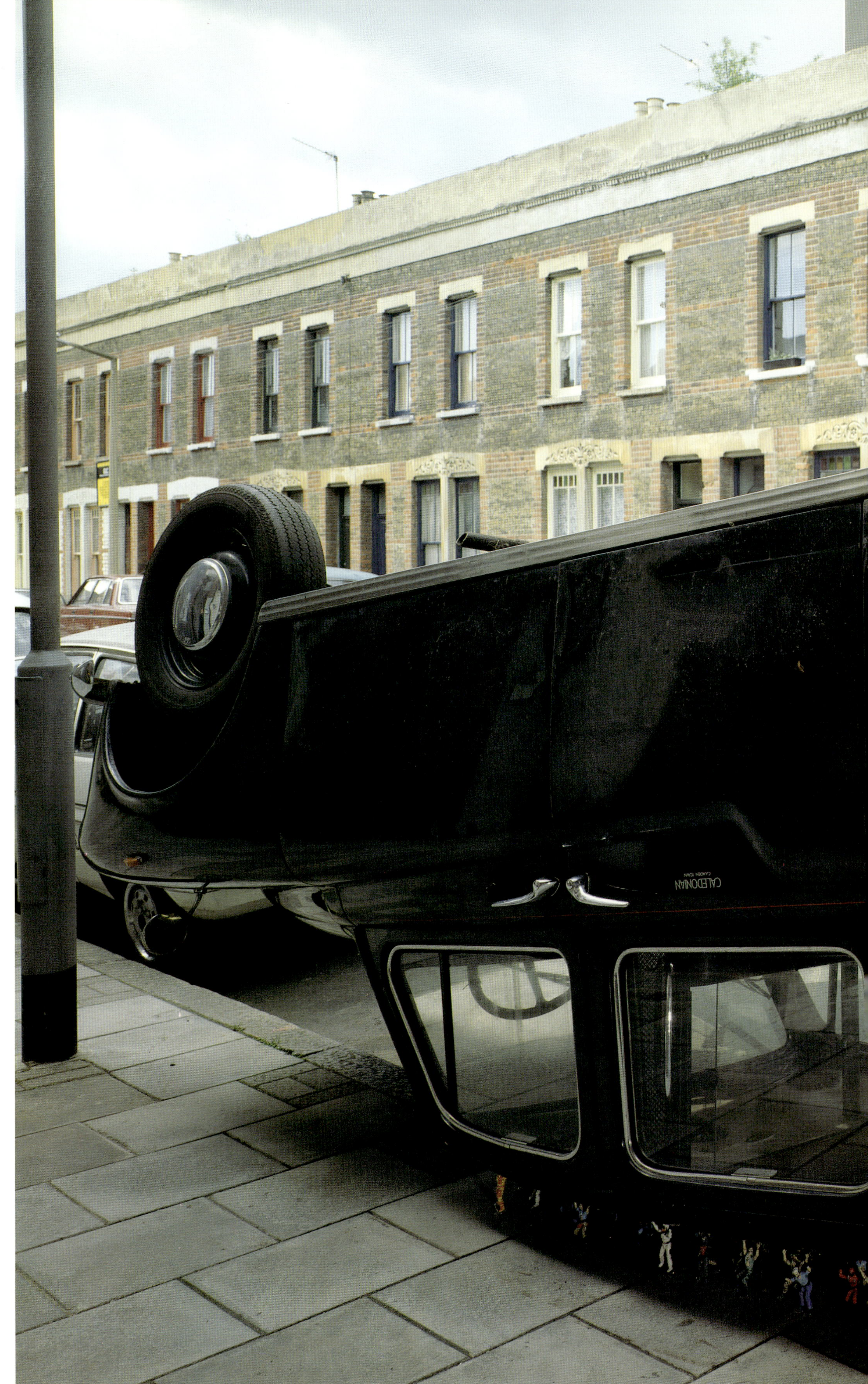

CALEDONIAN CAMDEN TOWN

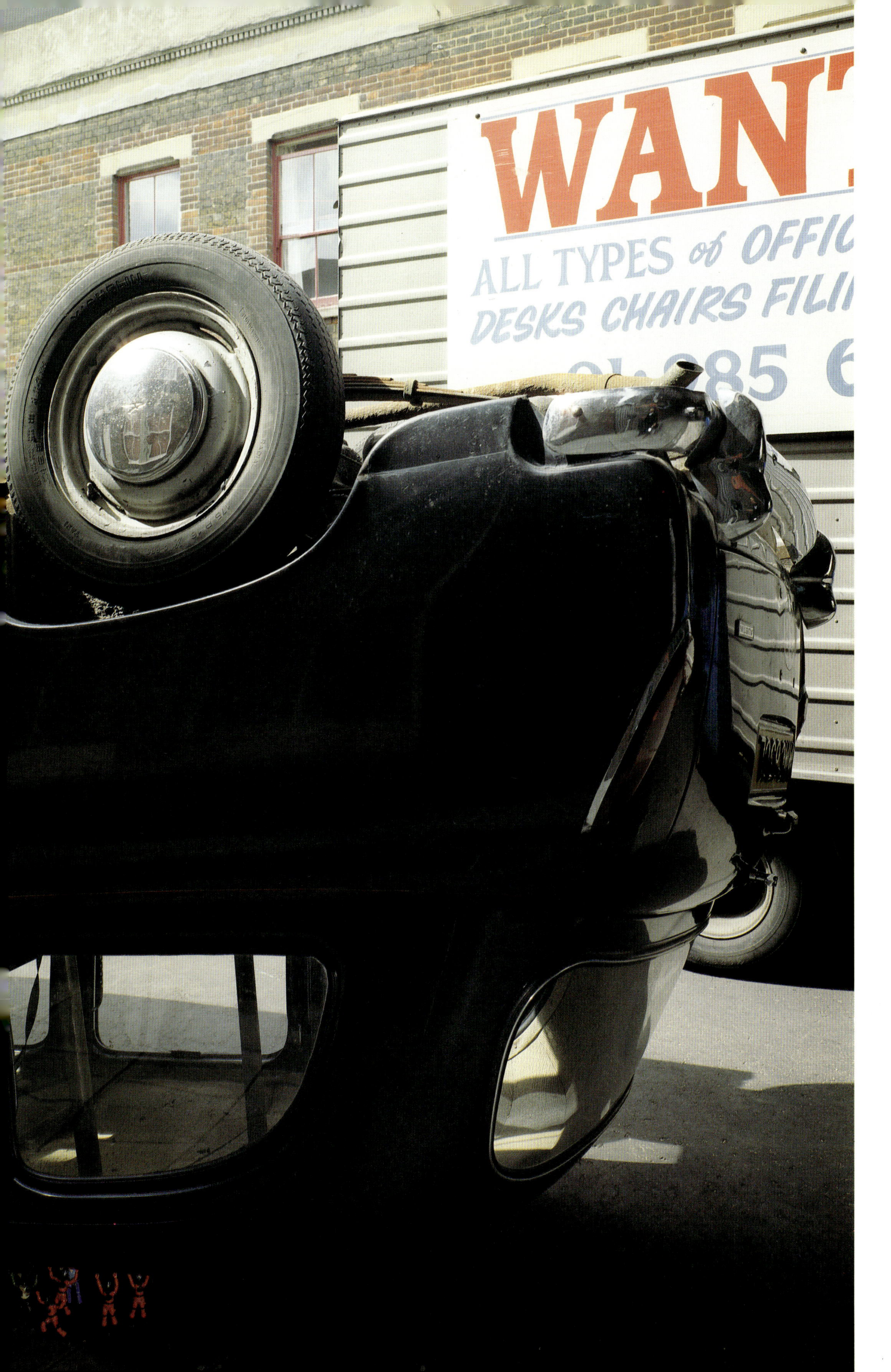

WAN
ALL TYPES of OFFIC
DESKS CHAIRS FILI
01 685 6

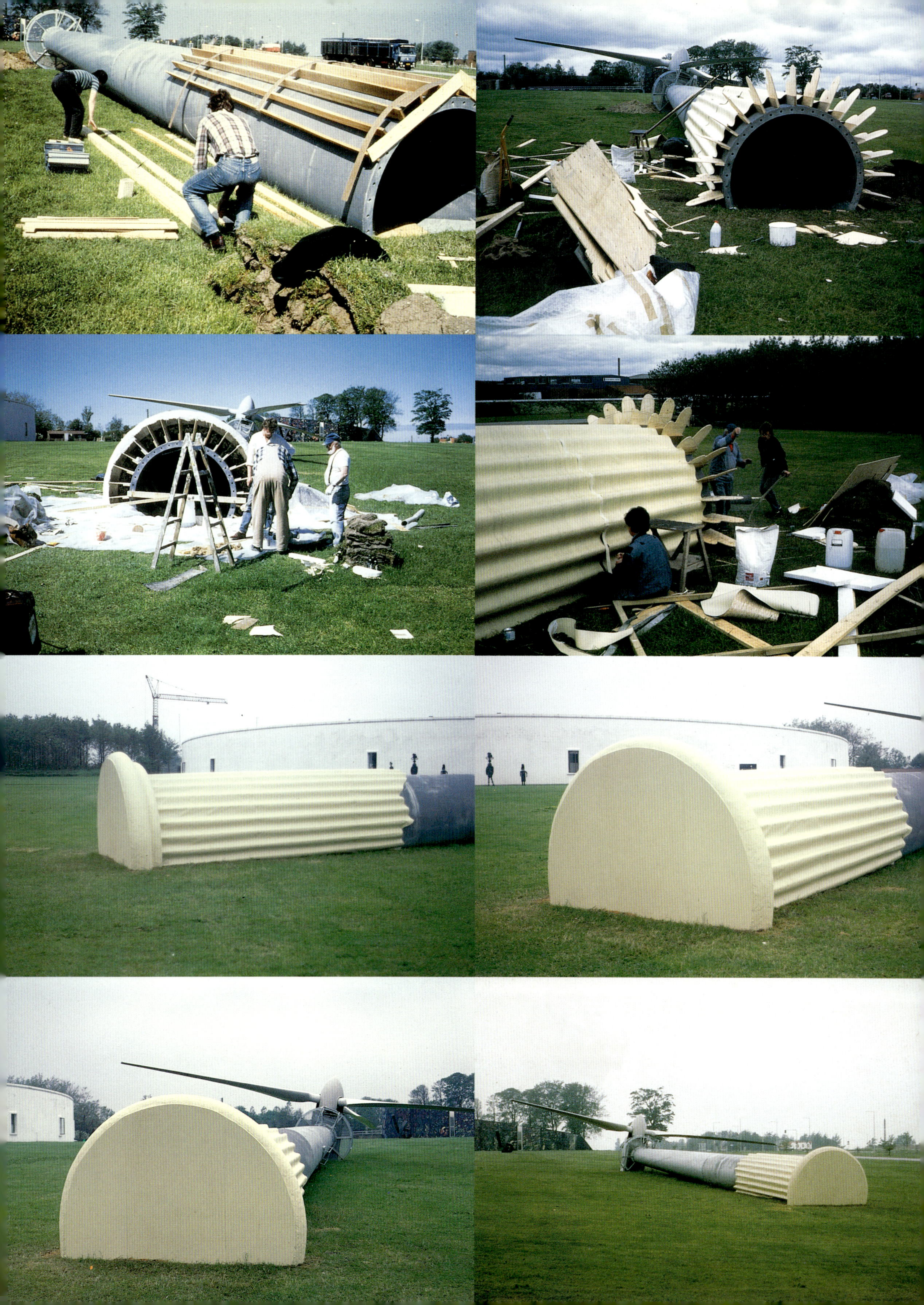

Opposite : UNTITLED / Herning Kunstmuseum, Herning, Denmark / June 1986 / Photographer - Rigmor Lovring

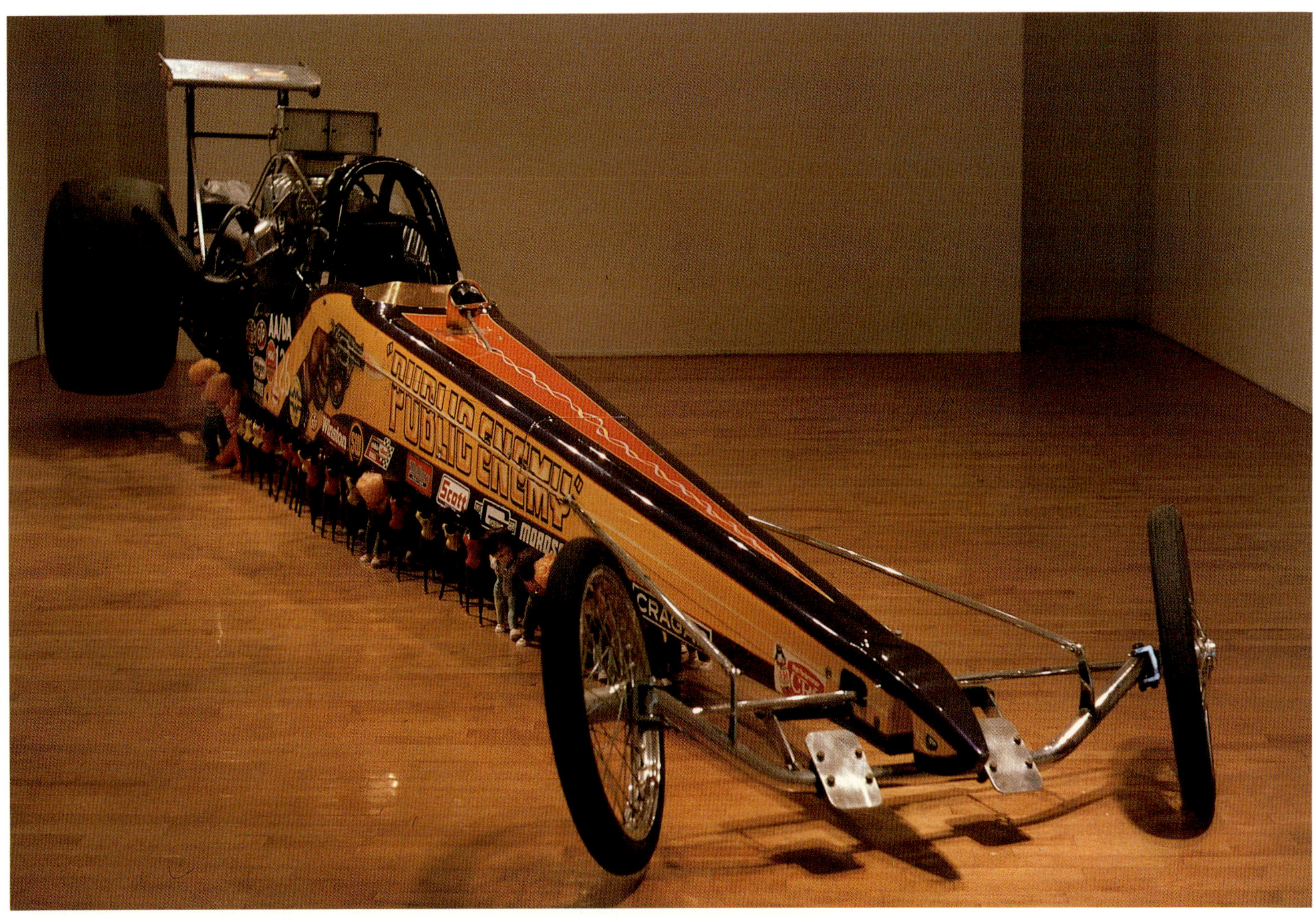

ROADSHOW / Barbara Toll Fine Art Inc, New York / April 1986 / Photographer - Garrard Martin

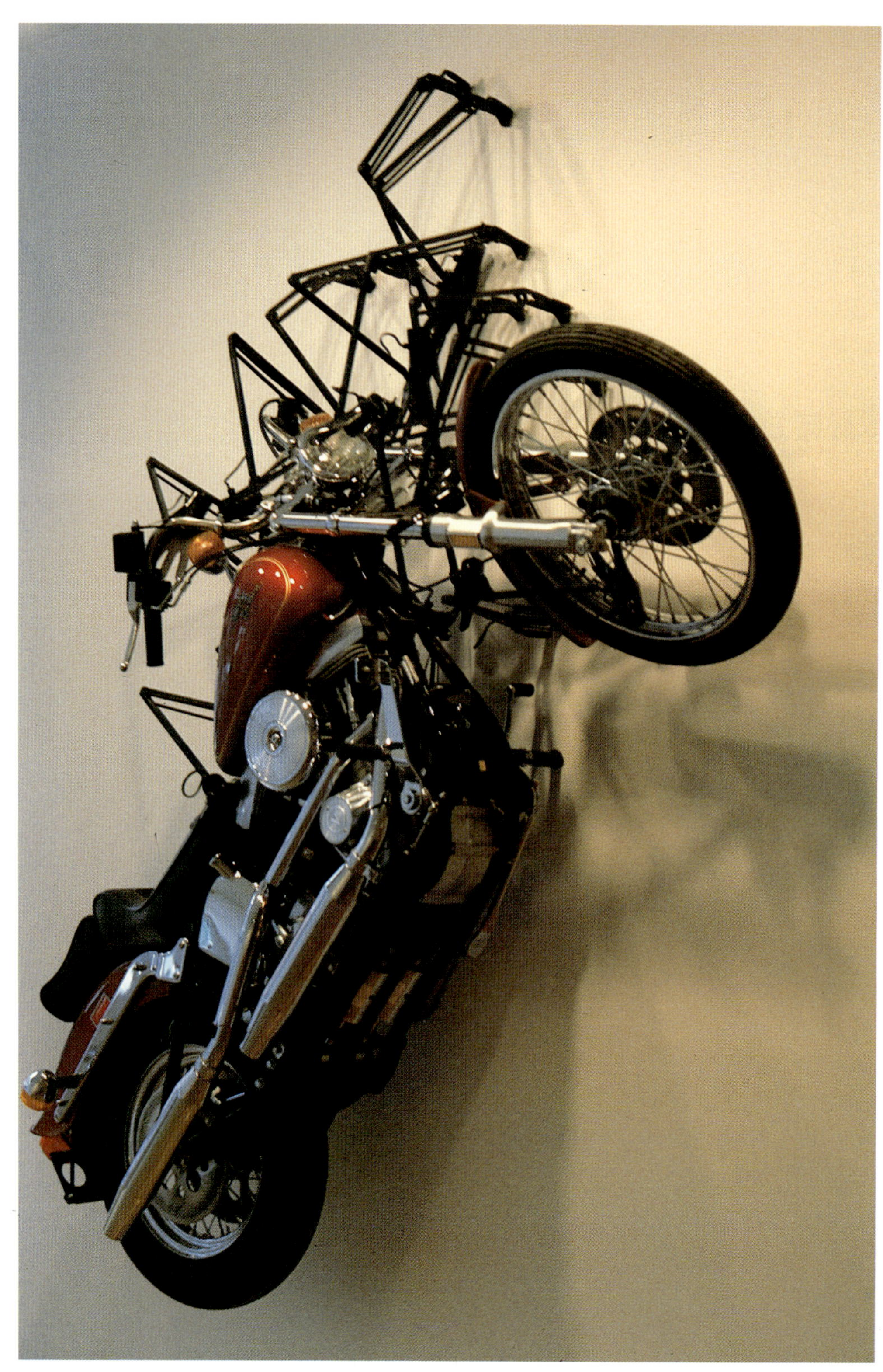

ROADSHOW / Barbara Toll Fine Art Inc, New York / April 1986

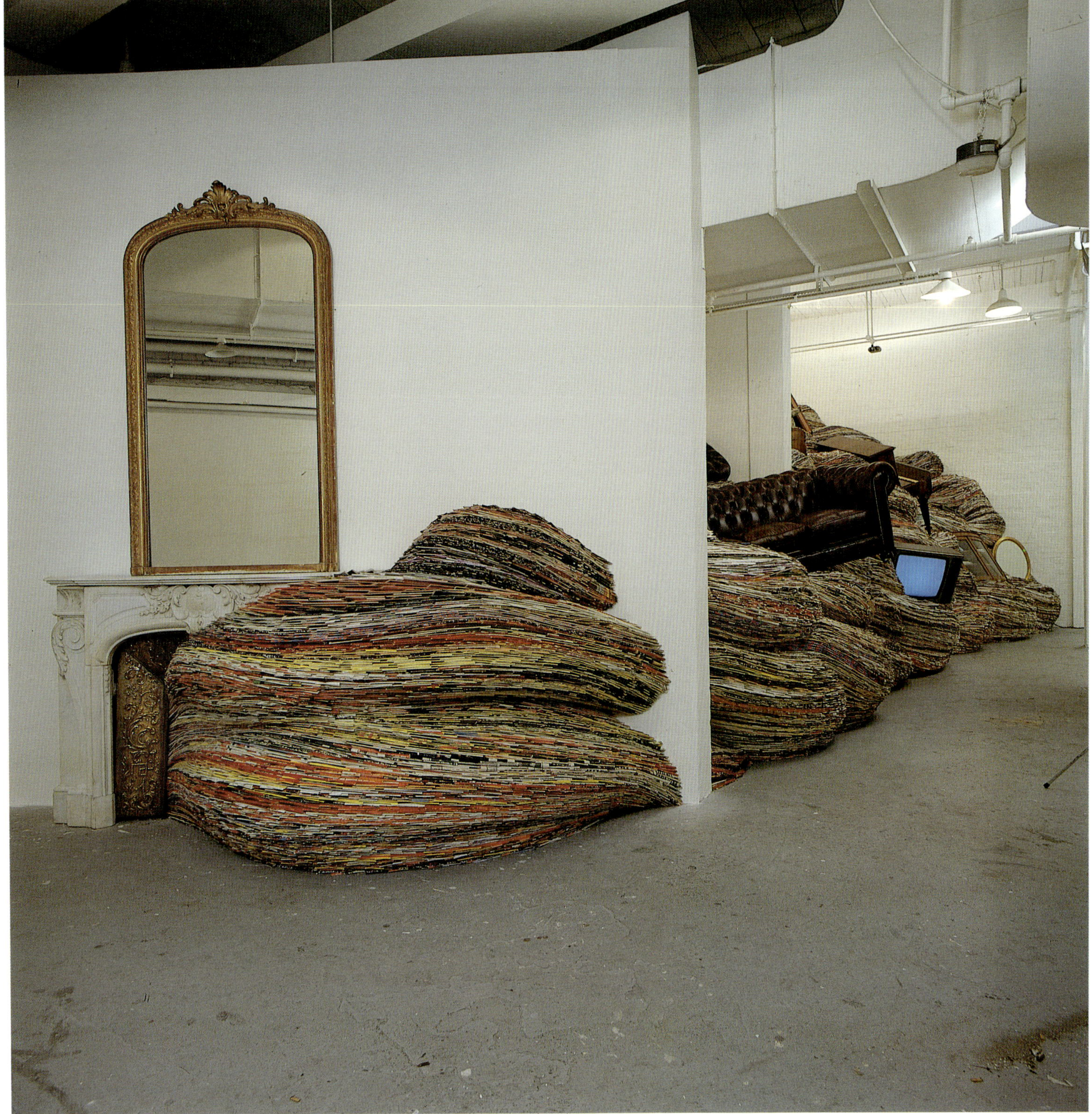

FUEL FOR THE FIRE / Riverside Studios, Hammersmith, London / August 1986 / Photographer - Edward Woodman

Following Page : FUEL FOR THE FIRE / Riverside Studios, Hammersmith, London / August 1986 / Photographer - Edward Woodman

IF YOU GO DOWN TO THE WOODS TO-DAY / Fundació Joan Miró, Barcelona / June 1987
Collection - Rafael Tous /Photographer - Ant Critchfield

P26-27 ADDING FUEL TO THE FIRE / Metronom Gallery, Barcelona / June 1987 / Photographer - Ant Critchfield

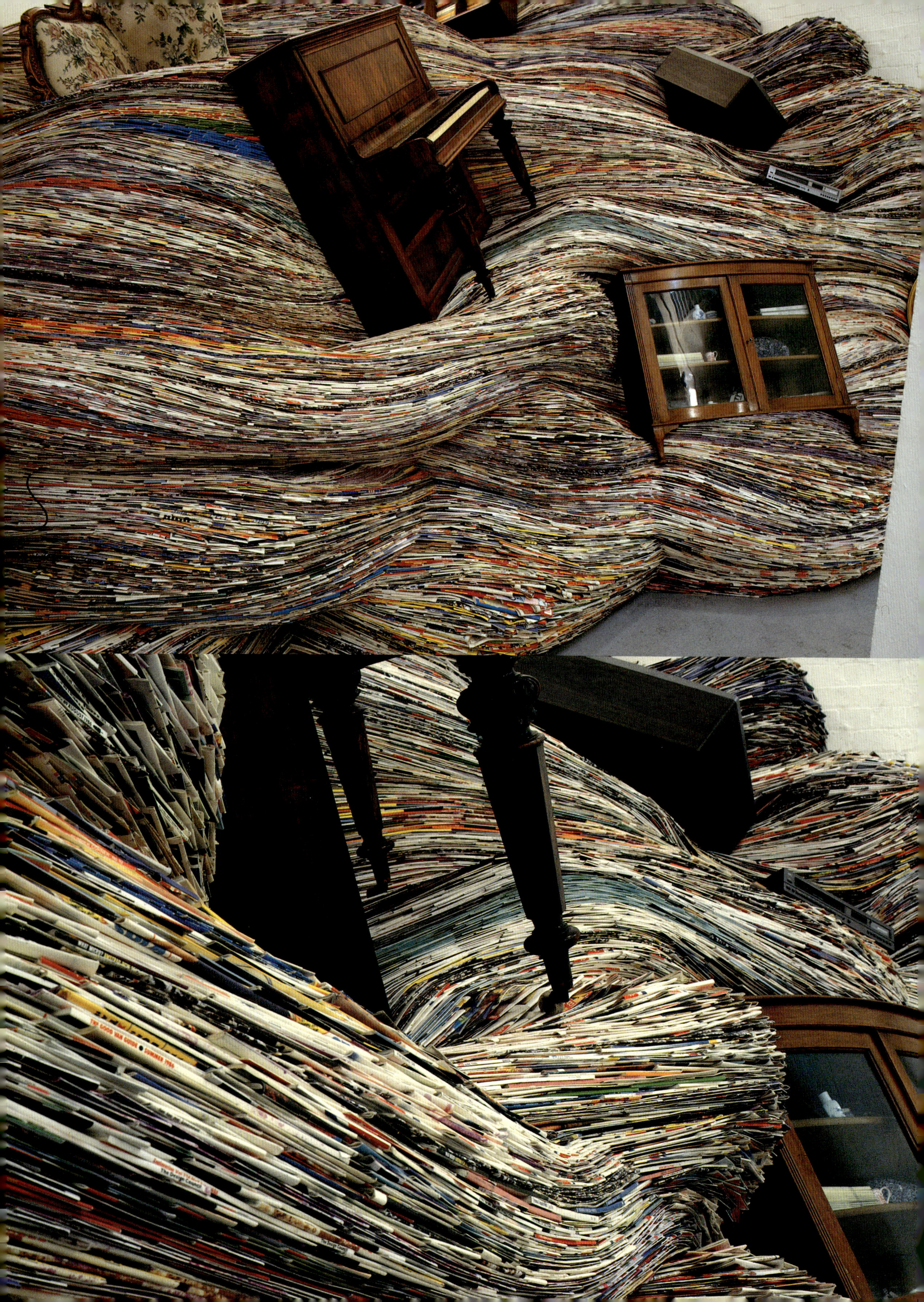

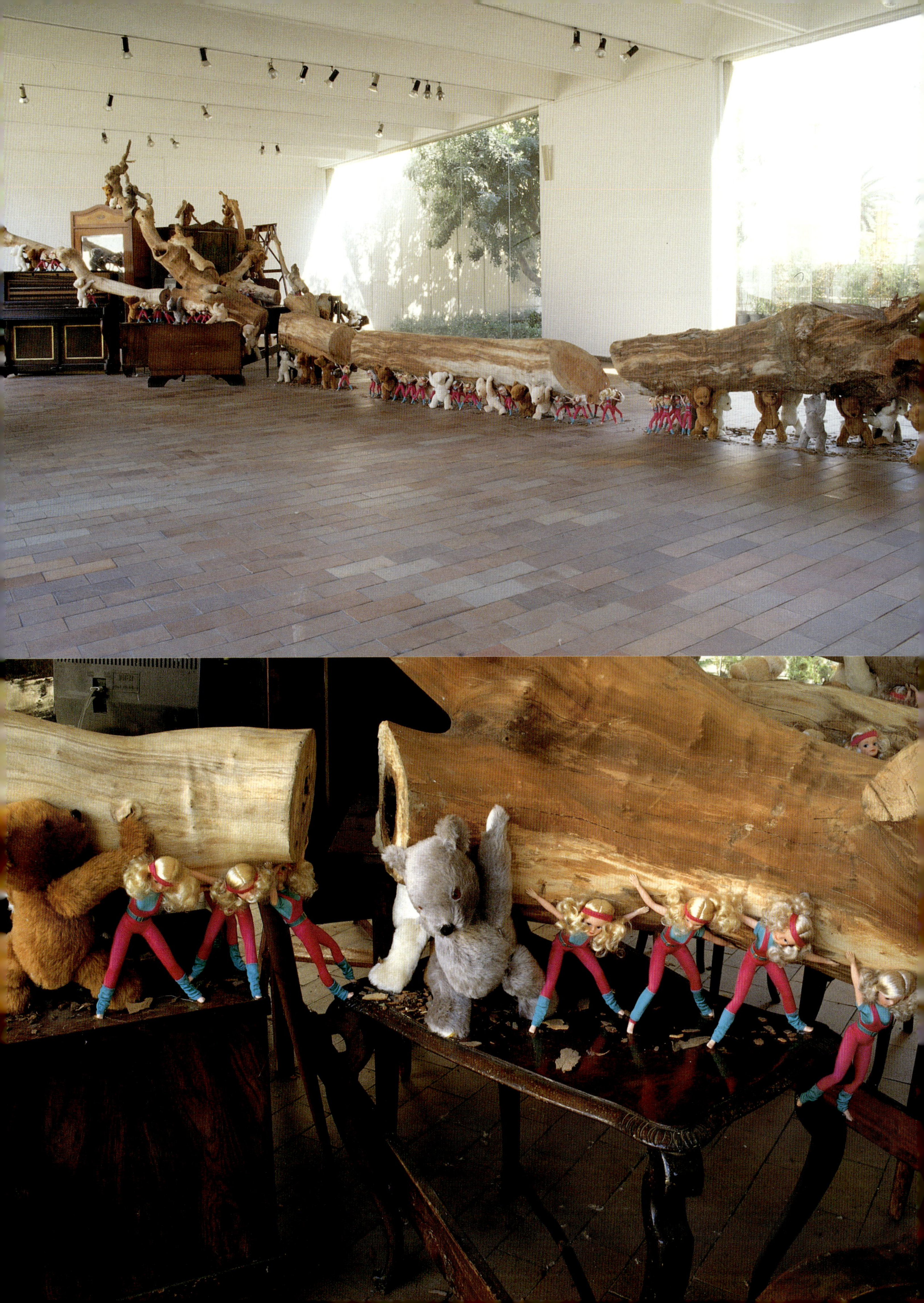

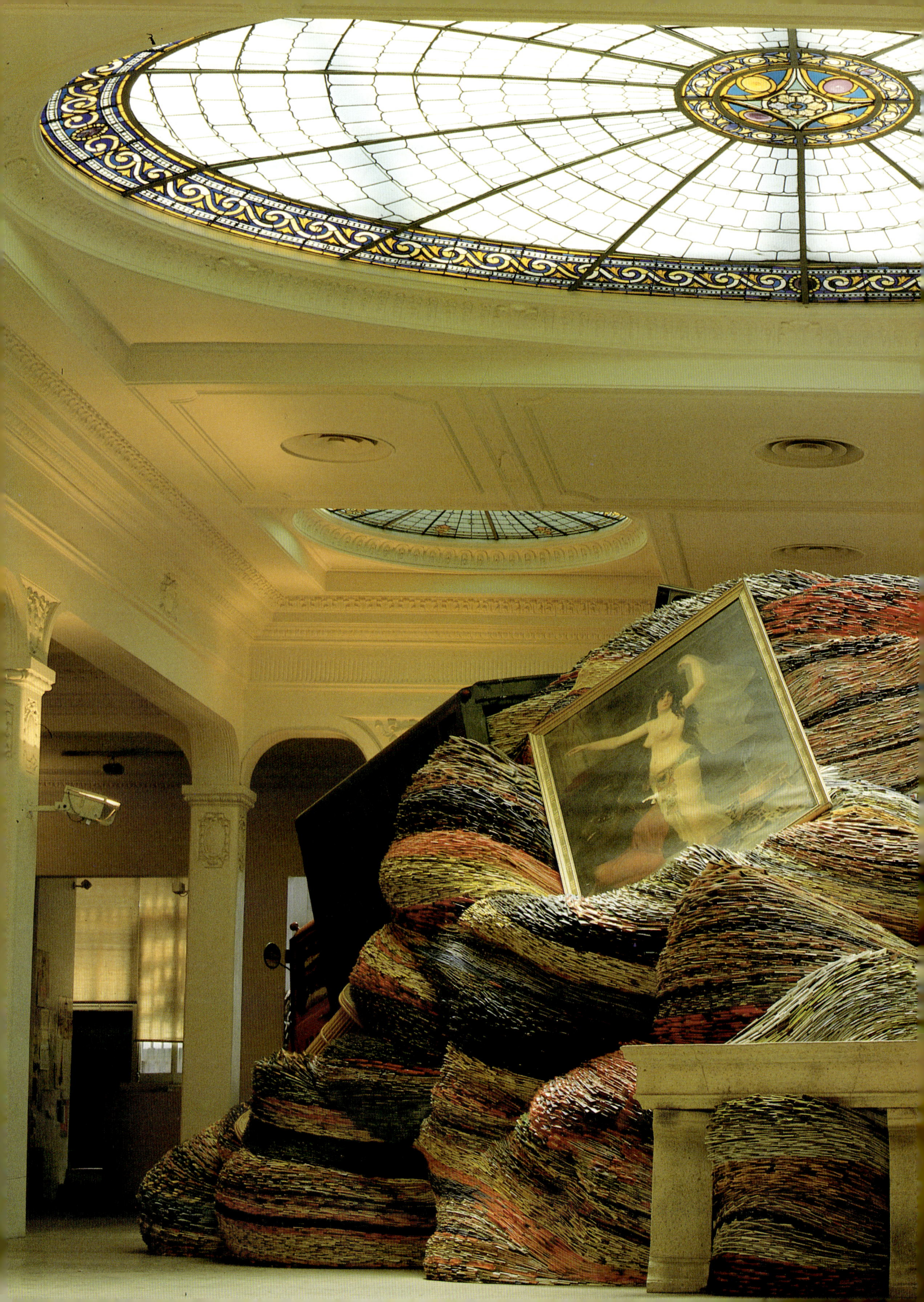

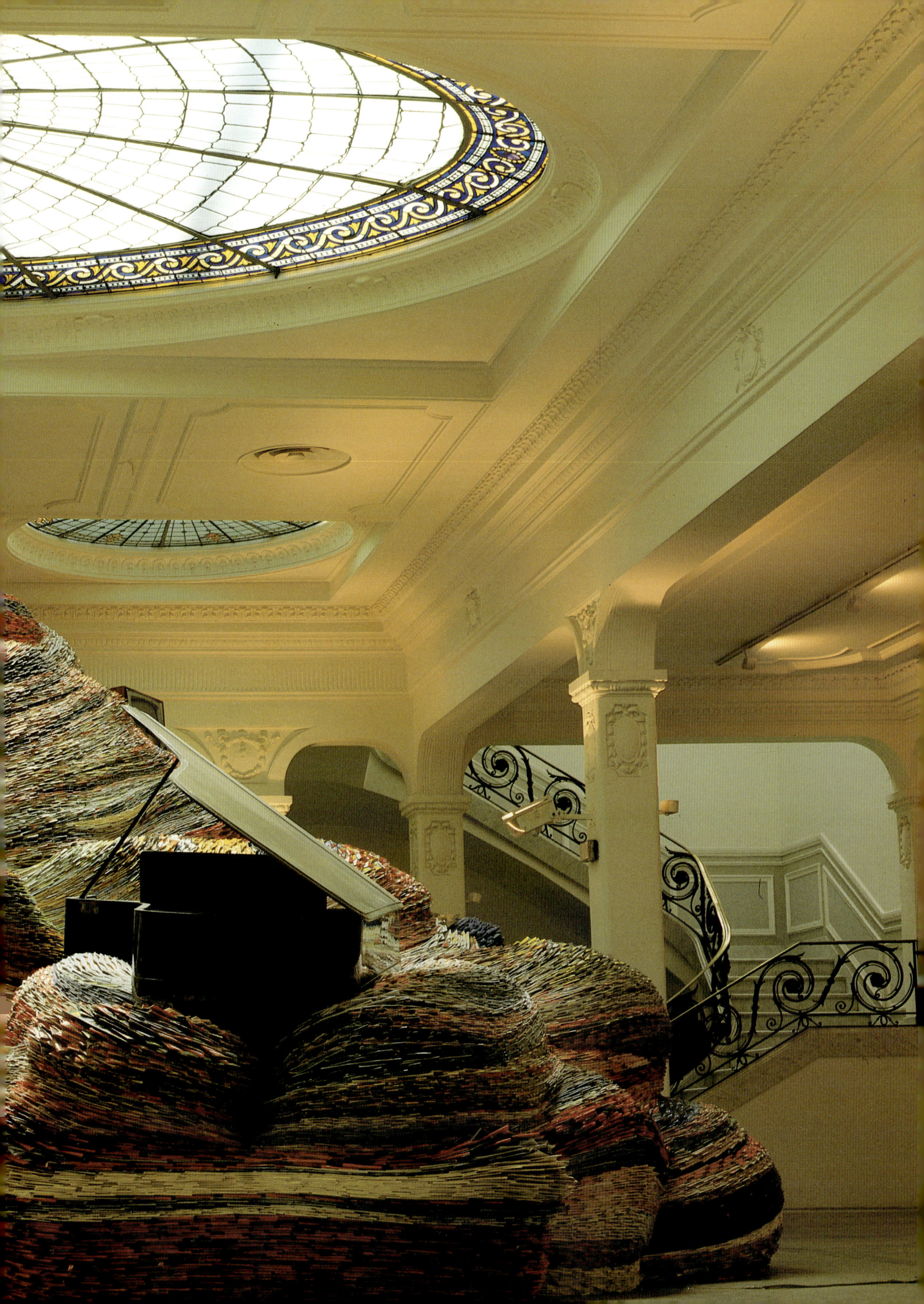

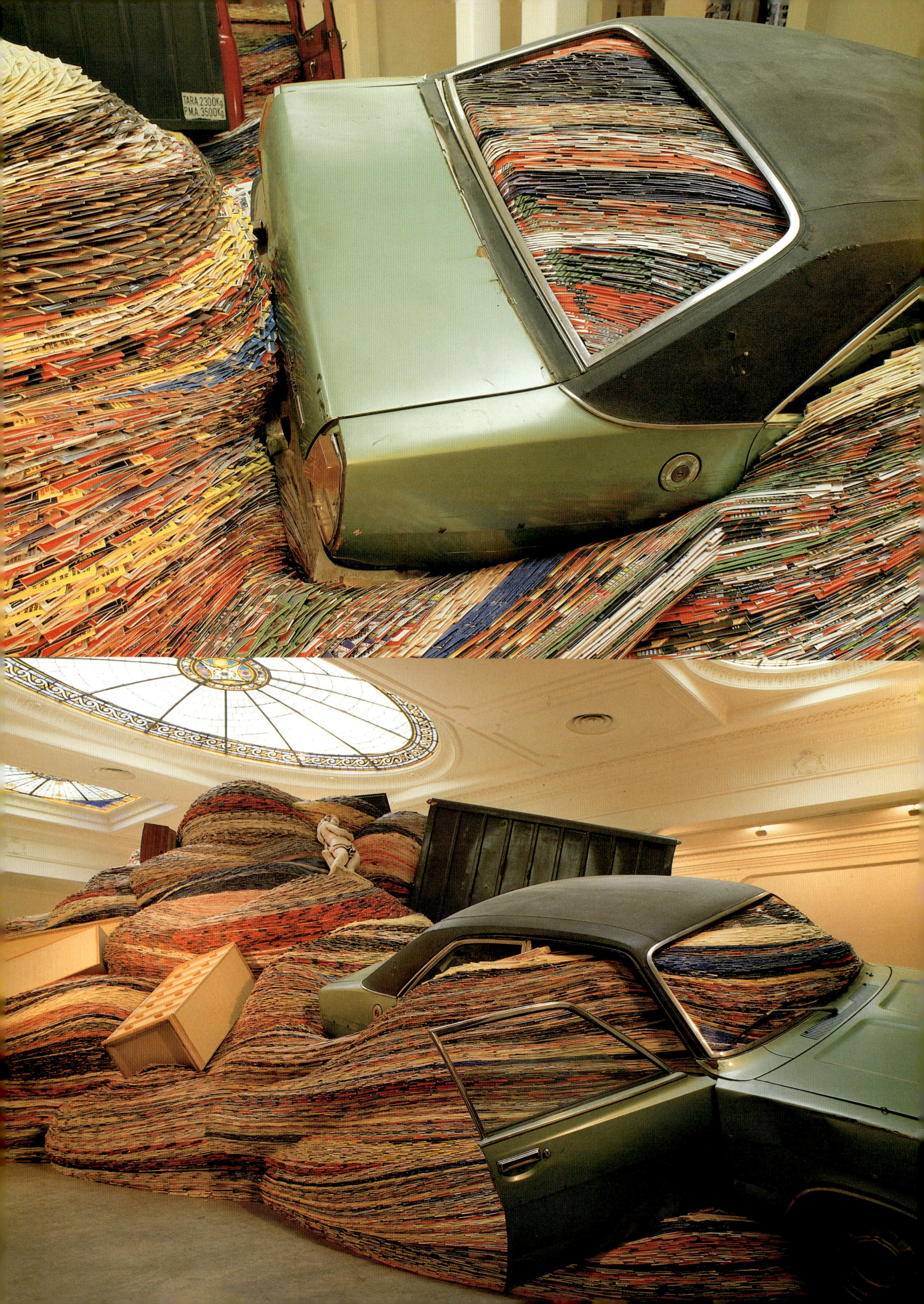

Opposite : ADDING FUEL TO THE FIRE / Metronom Gallery, Barcelona / June 1987 / Photographer - Ant Critchfield

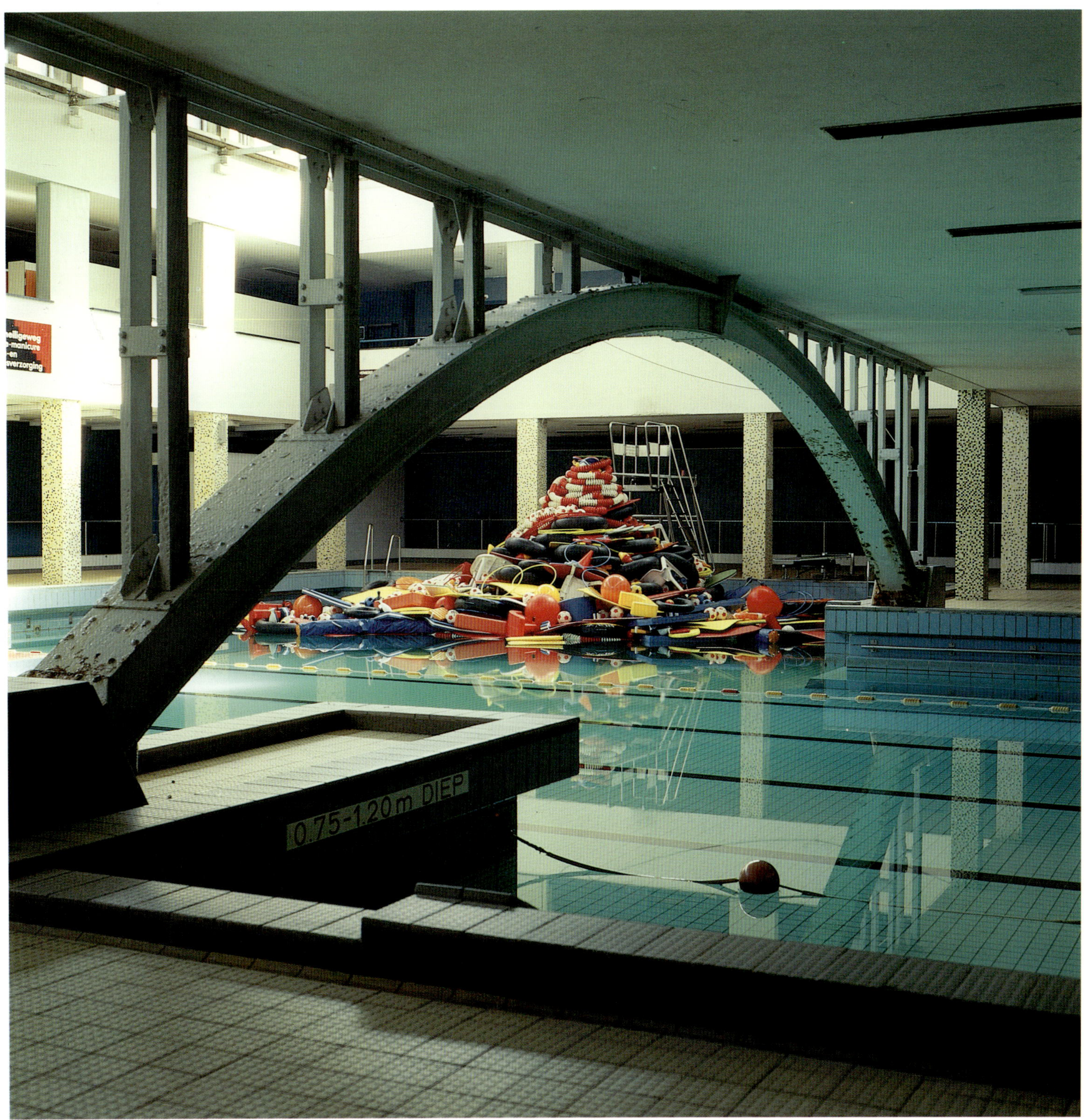

HIGH & DRY / Century 87, Heiligewegbad, Amsterdam / August 1987 / Photographer - Jannes Hinders

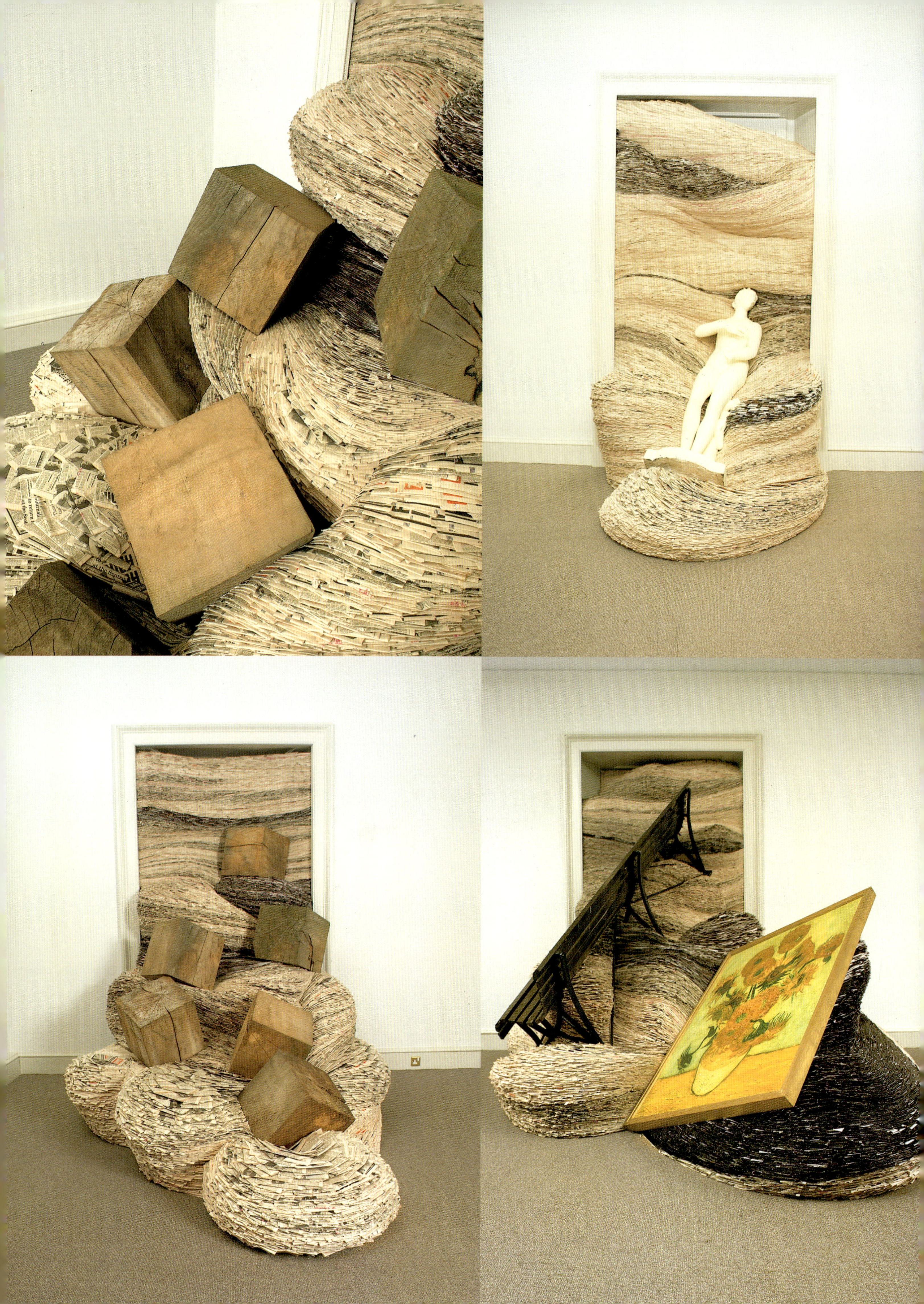

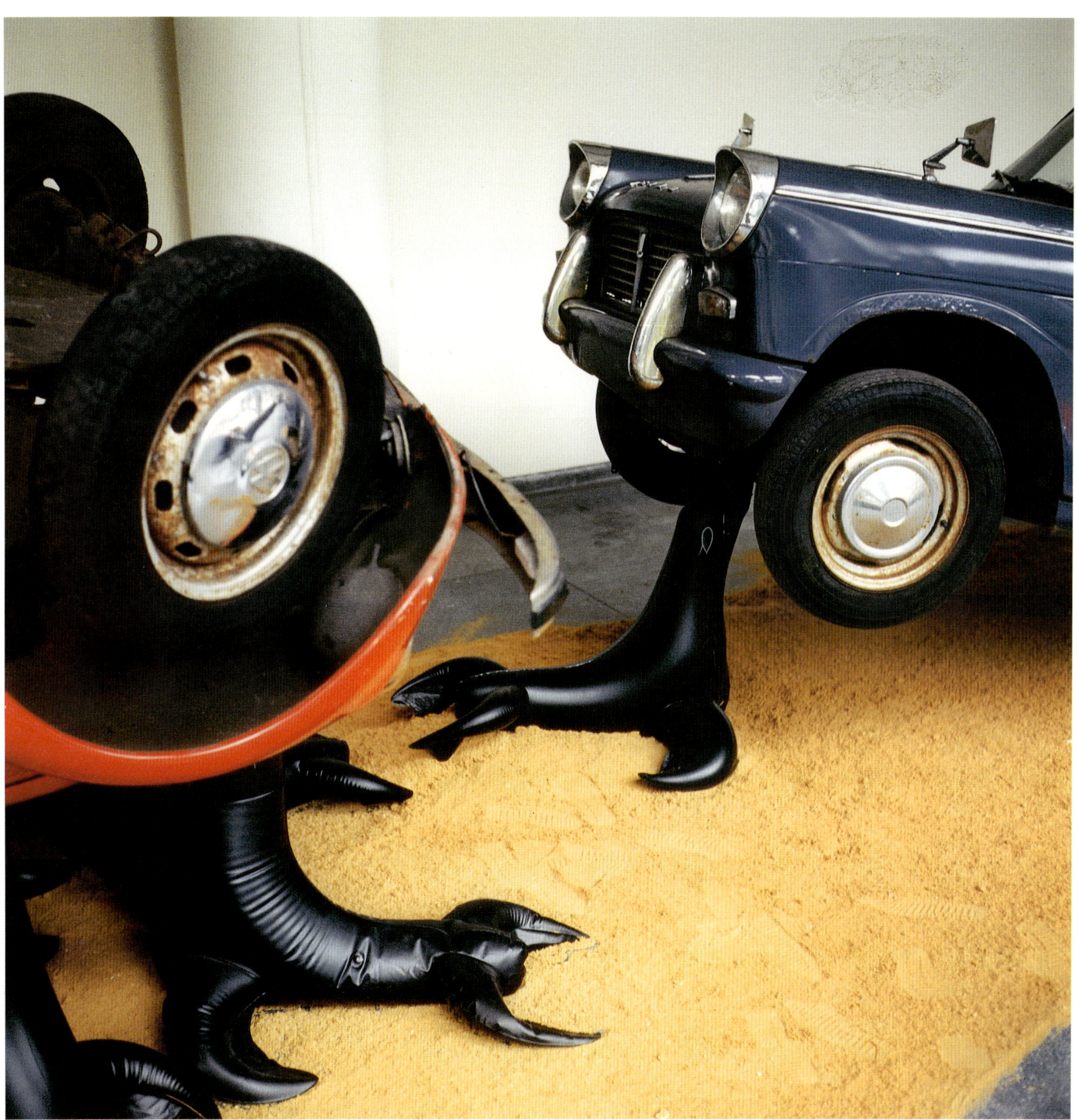

ANIMATED SUSPENSION / METAL AND MOTION / Brighton / September 1987 / Photographer - Ant Critchfield

Following Page : NATURAL CAUSES / Wiener Sezession, Vienna / September 1987 / Photo credit - Liesl Biber

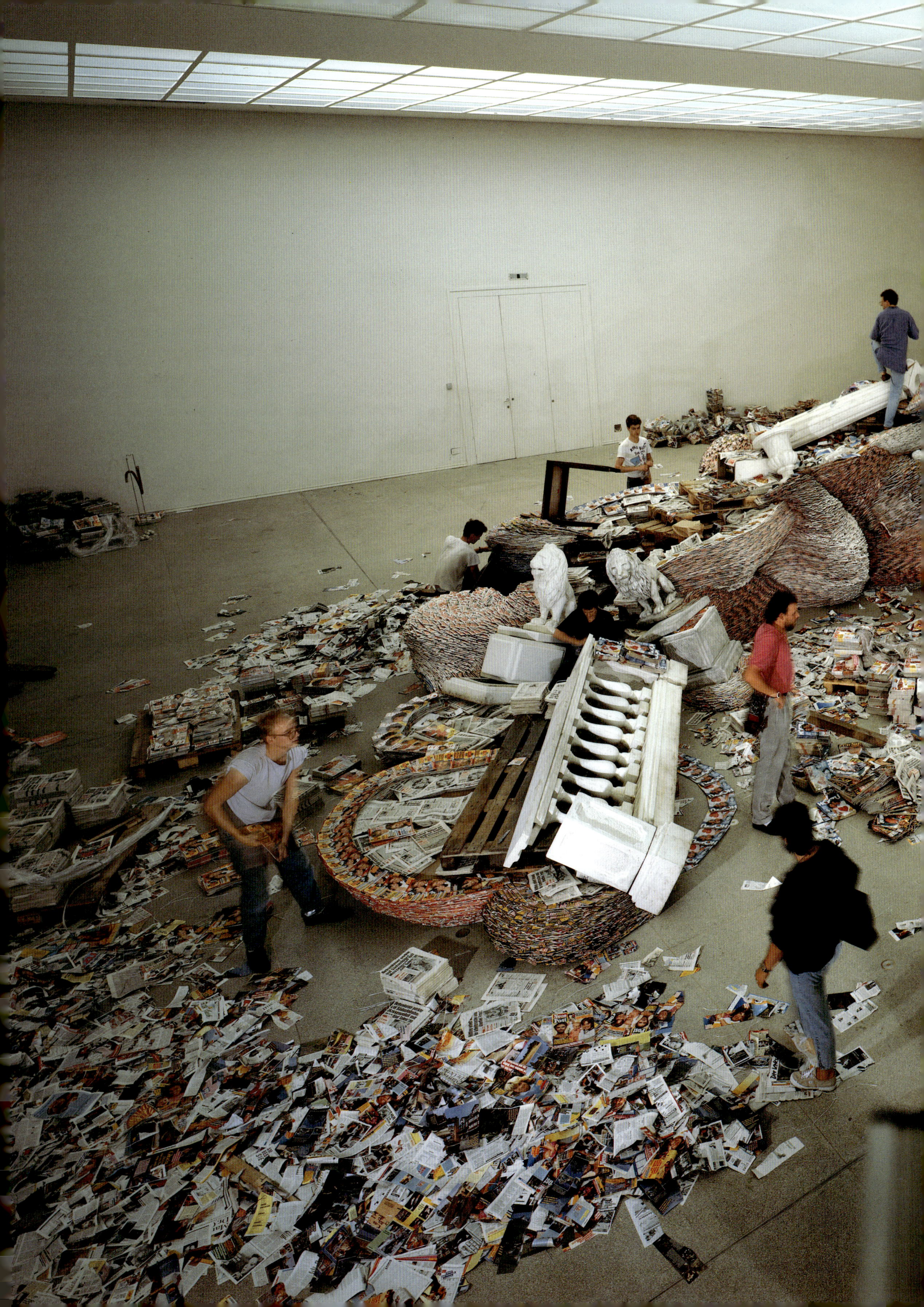

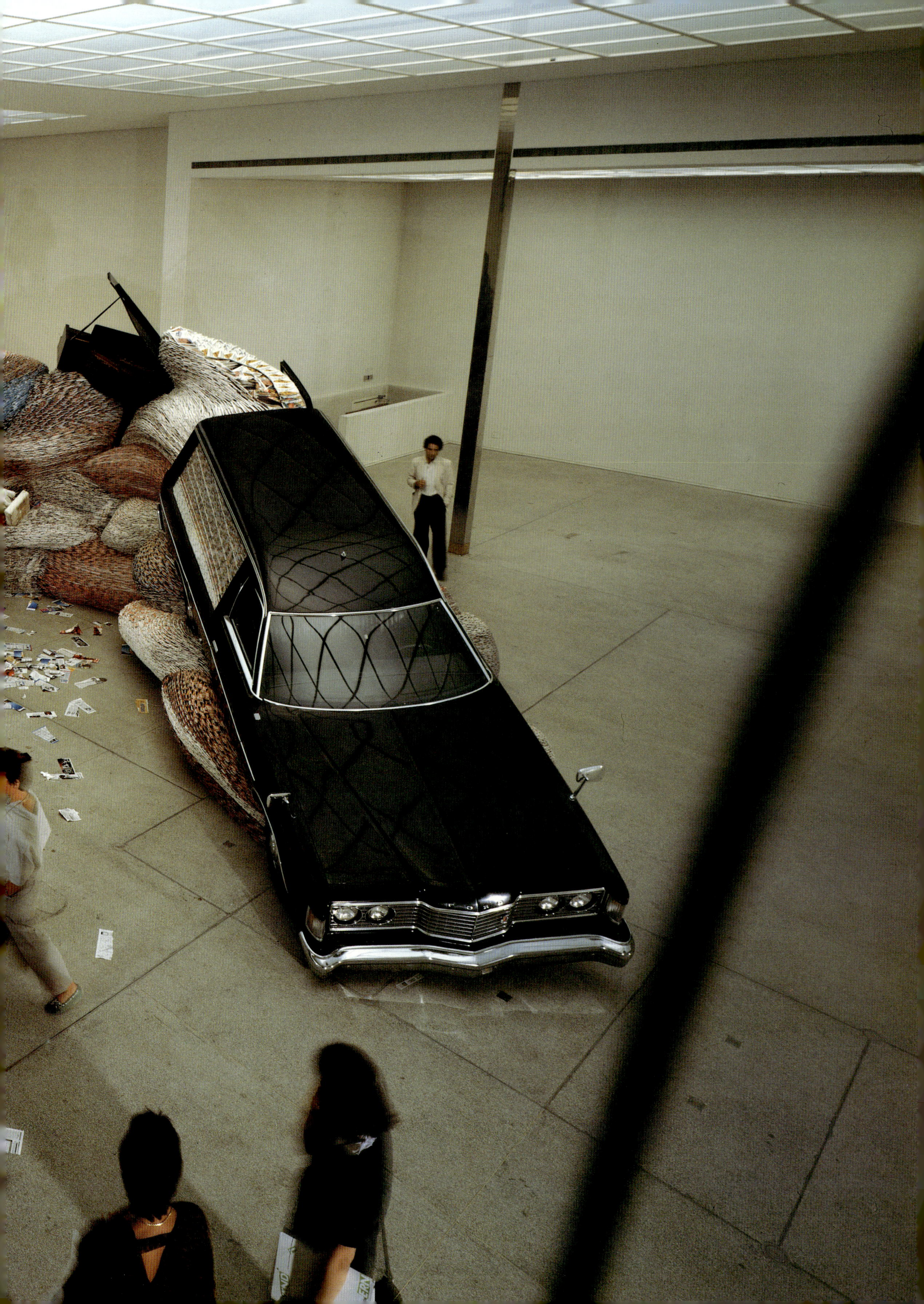

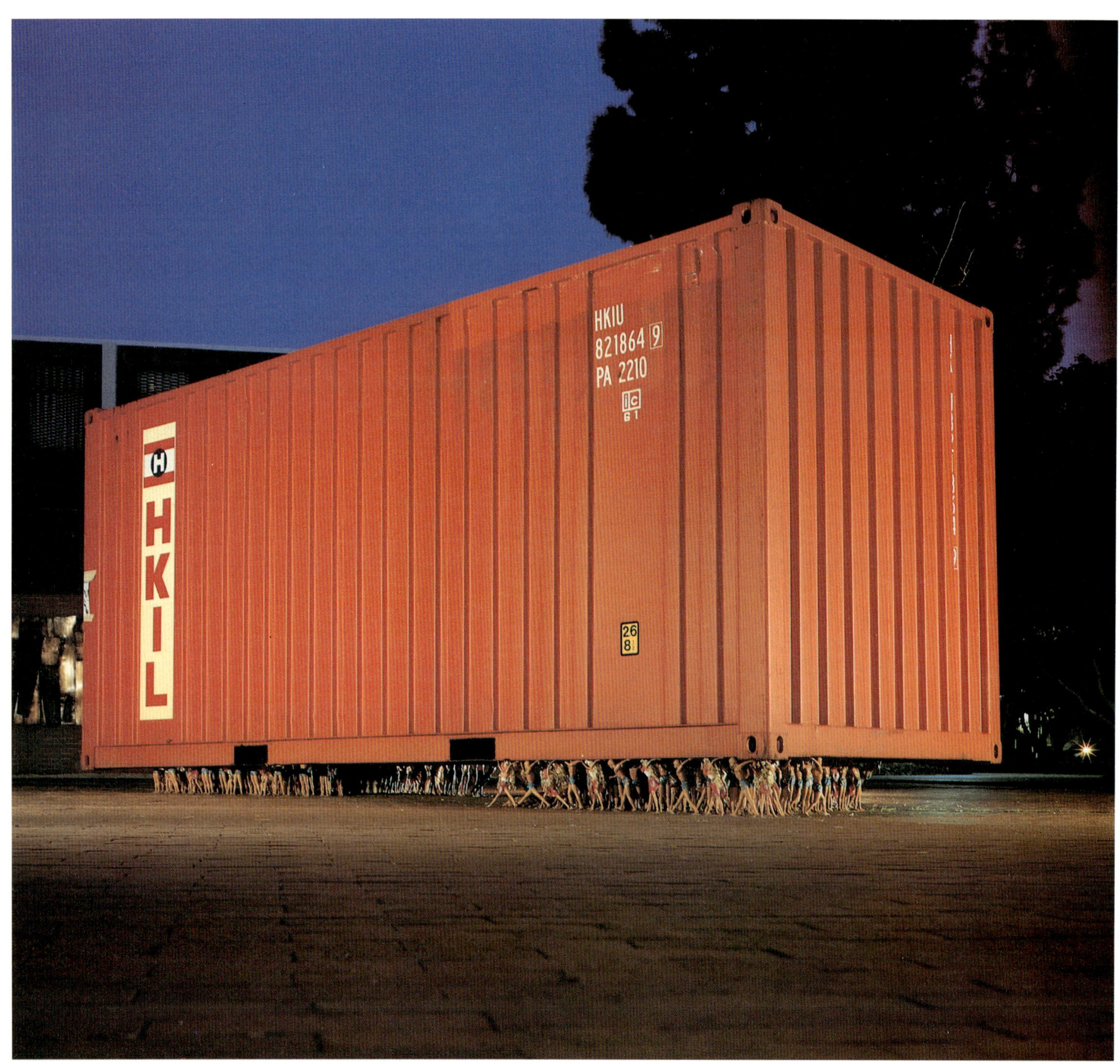

OFF THE BEATEN TRACK / U.K./L.A. Festival, U.C.L.A., Los Angeles / February 1988

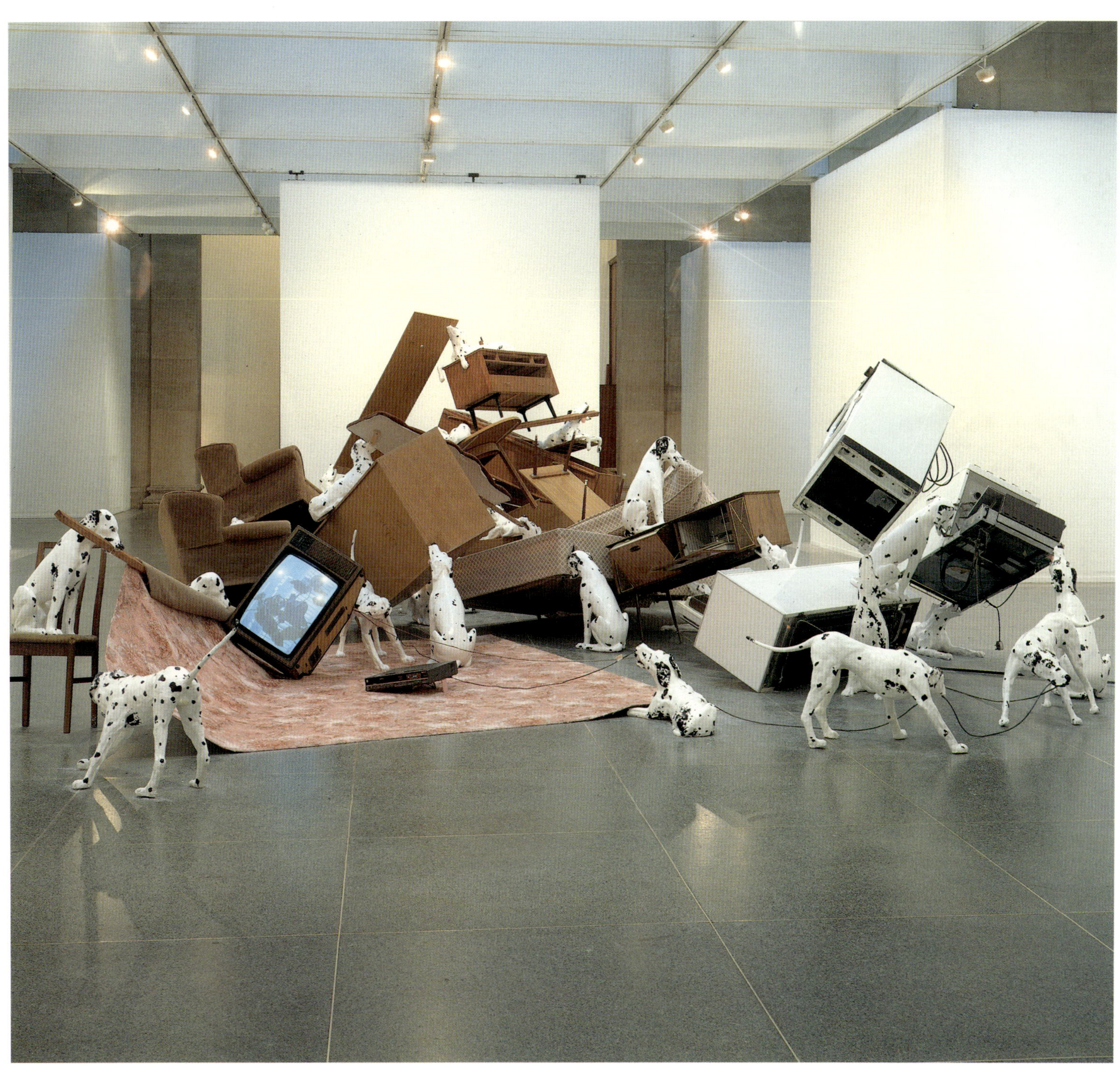

101 DALMATIONS / Tate Gallery, London / March 1988

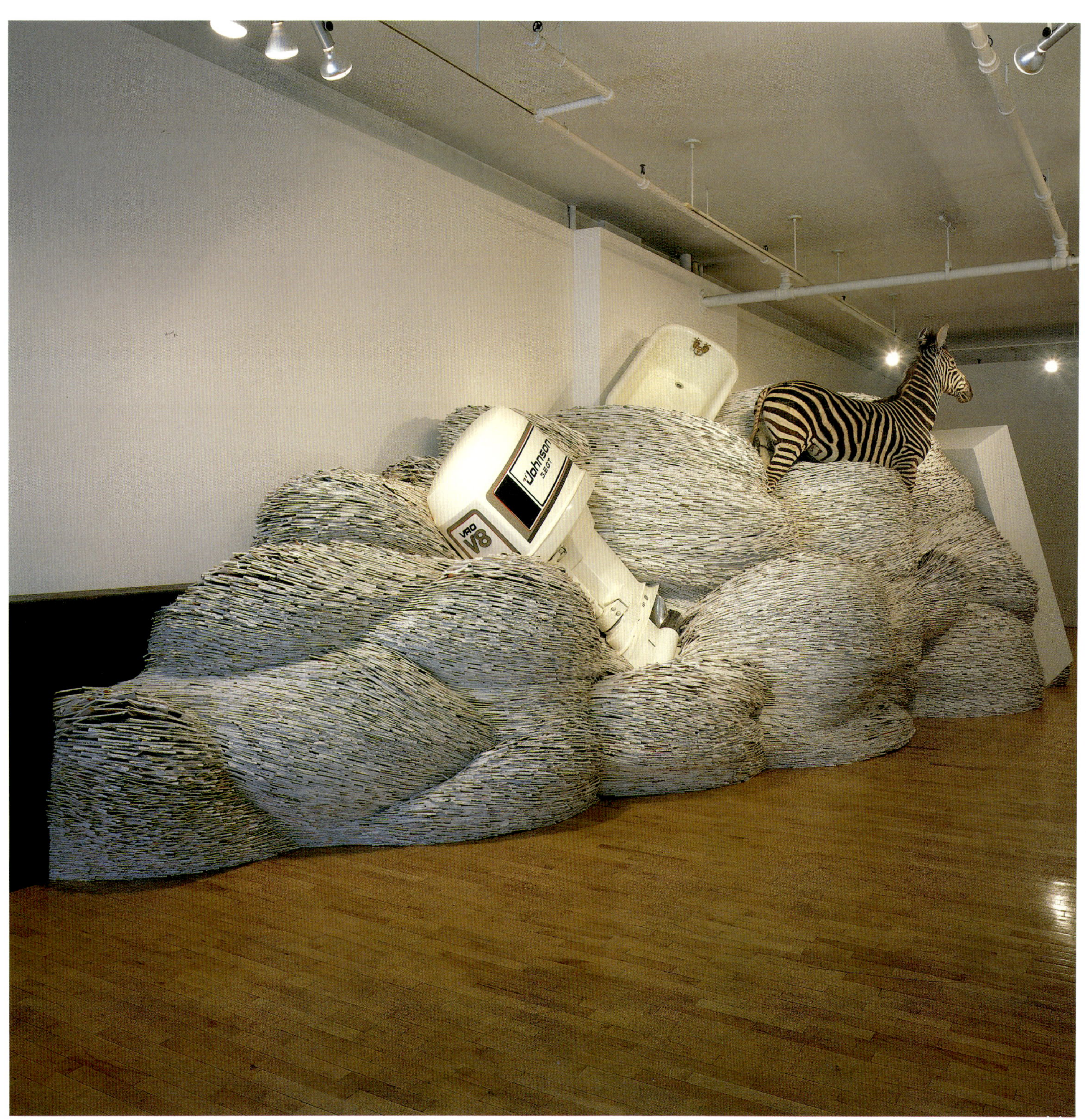

A MILLION MILES AWAY / Barbara Toll Fine Art Inc, New York / May 1988 / Photo - Zindman / Fremont

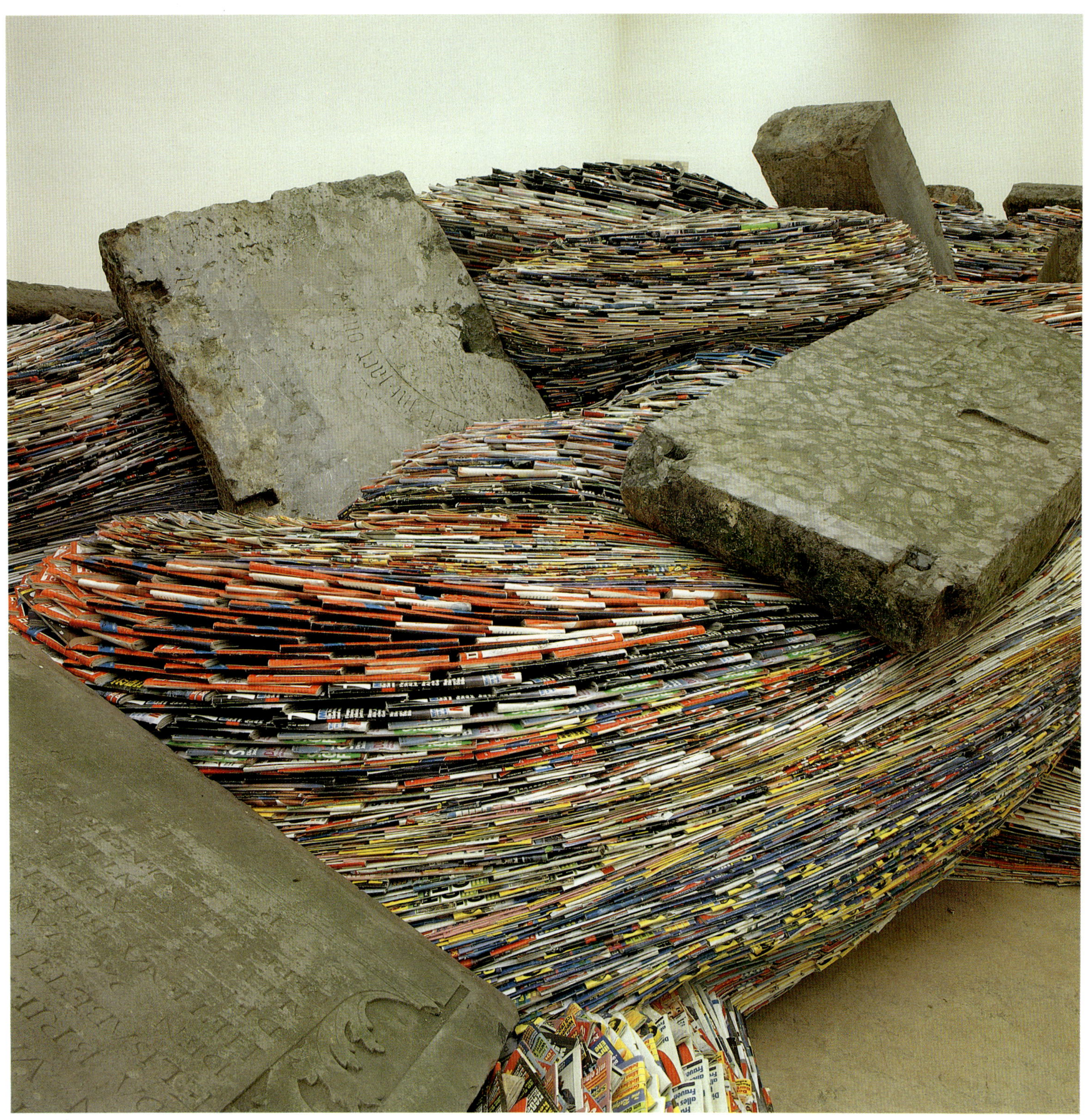

SIGNS OF LIFE / Provinciaal Museum of Hasselt, Hasselt, Belgium / May 1988

Following Page : MULTI-STORY CAR PARK / BBC Television Centre, London / May 1988 / Photographer - the Artist

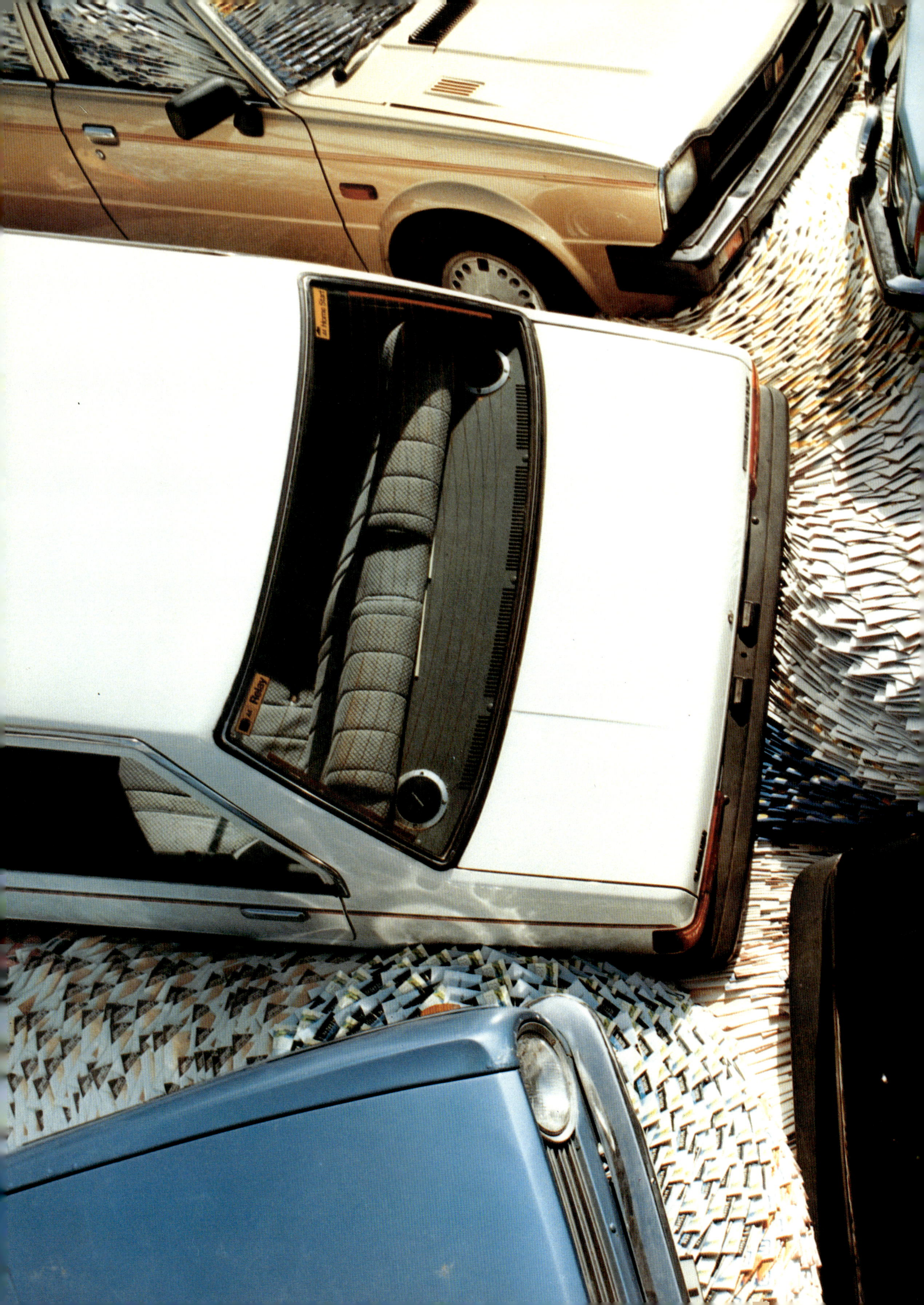

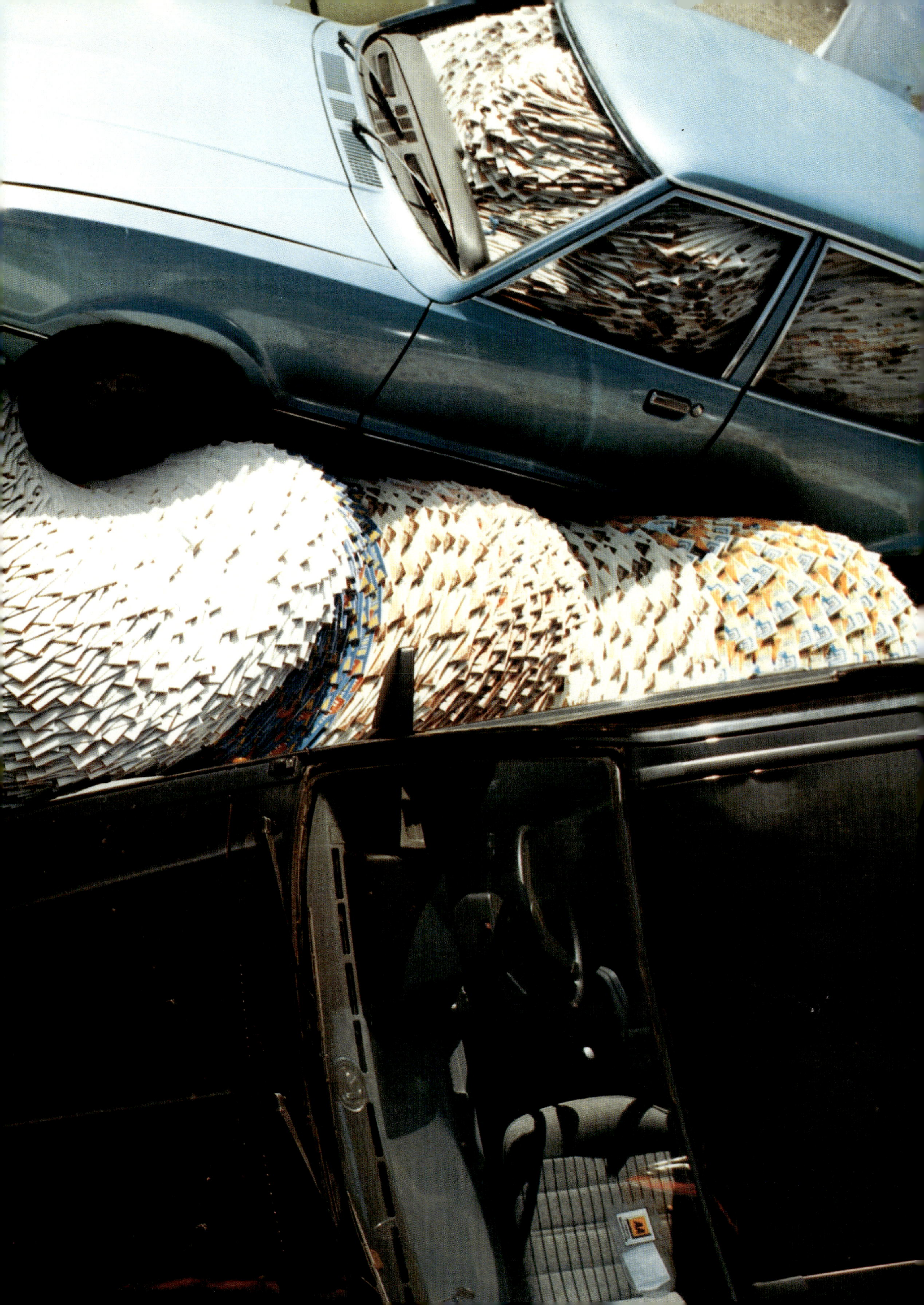

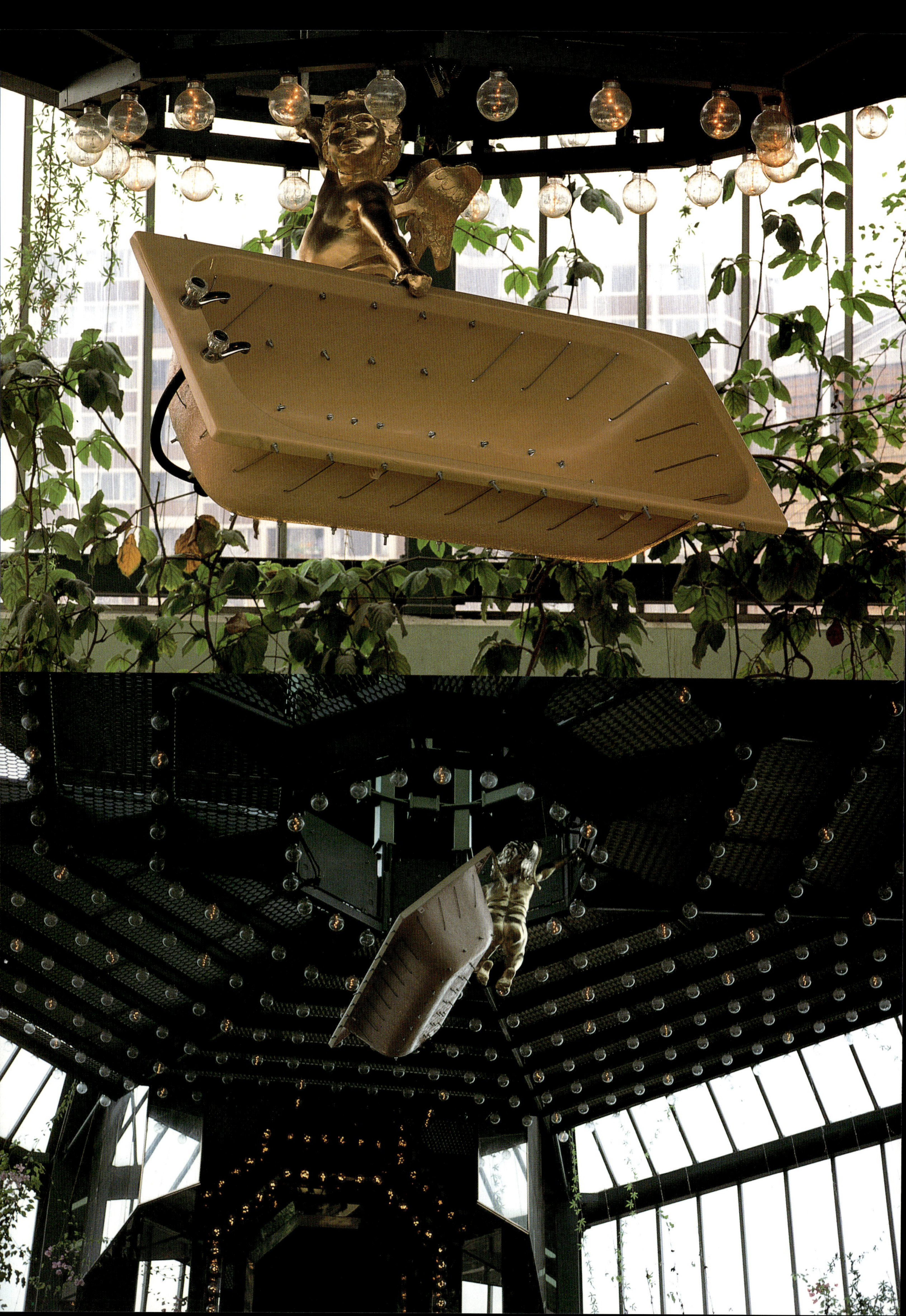

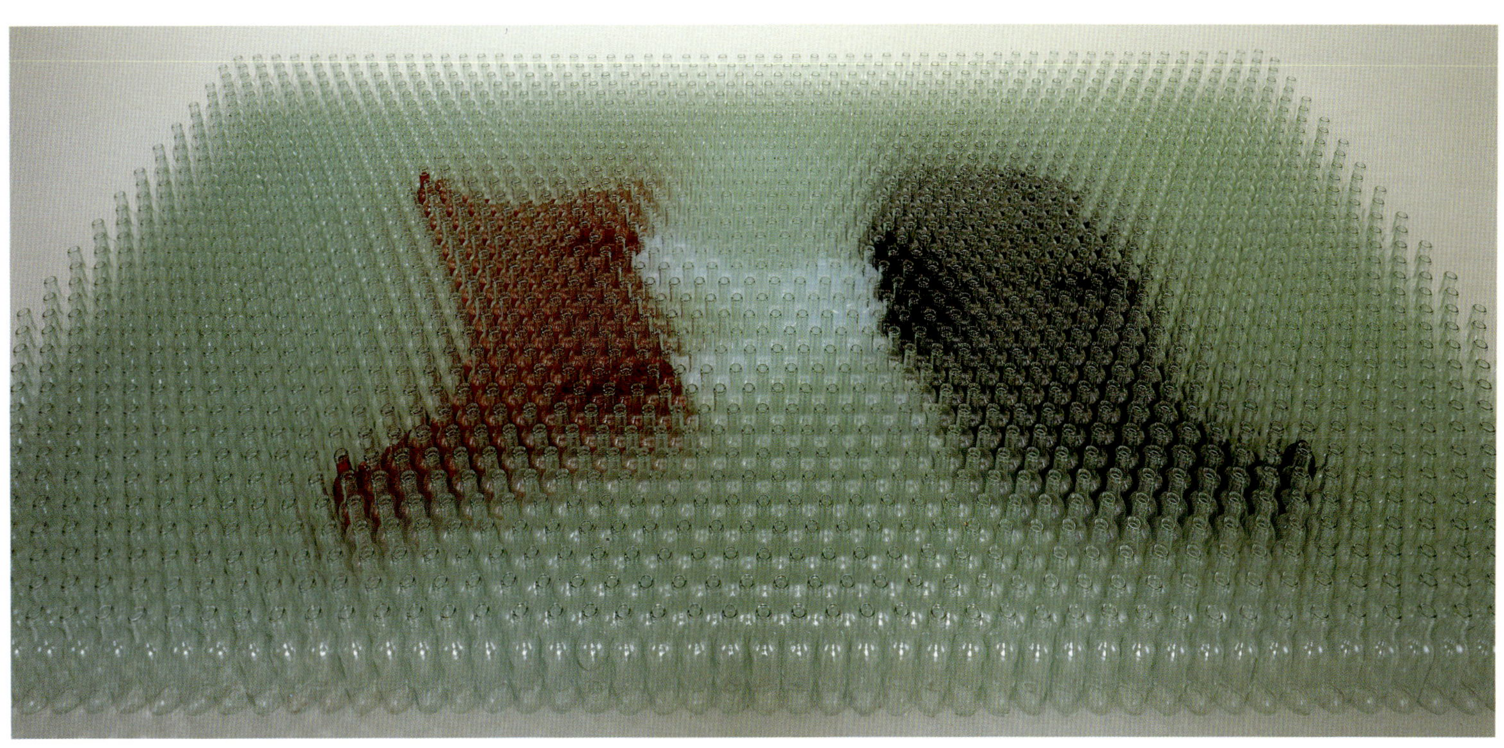

FUCKING FOR FRANCE / Galerie Ek'Ymose, Bordeaux / October 1988 / Photographer - Alain Beguerie

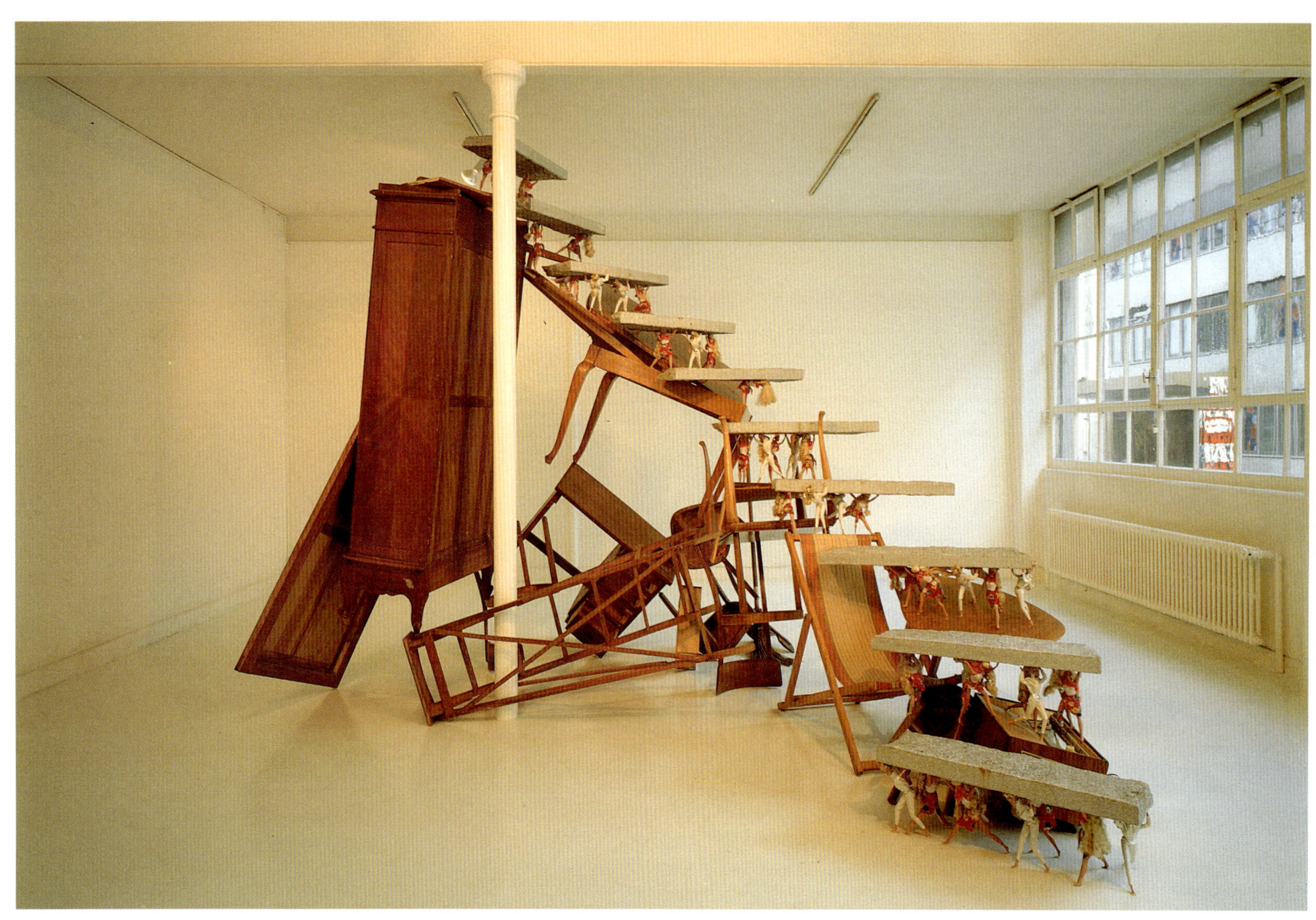

NO REST FOR THE WICKED / Galerie Andata/Ritorno, Geneva / November 1988 / Photo - Jaques Berthet / Collection - Sistovari

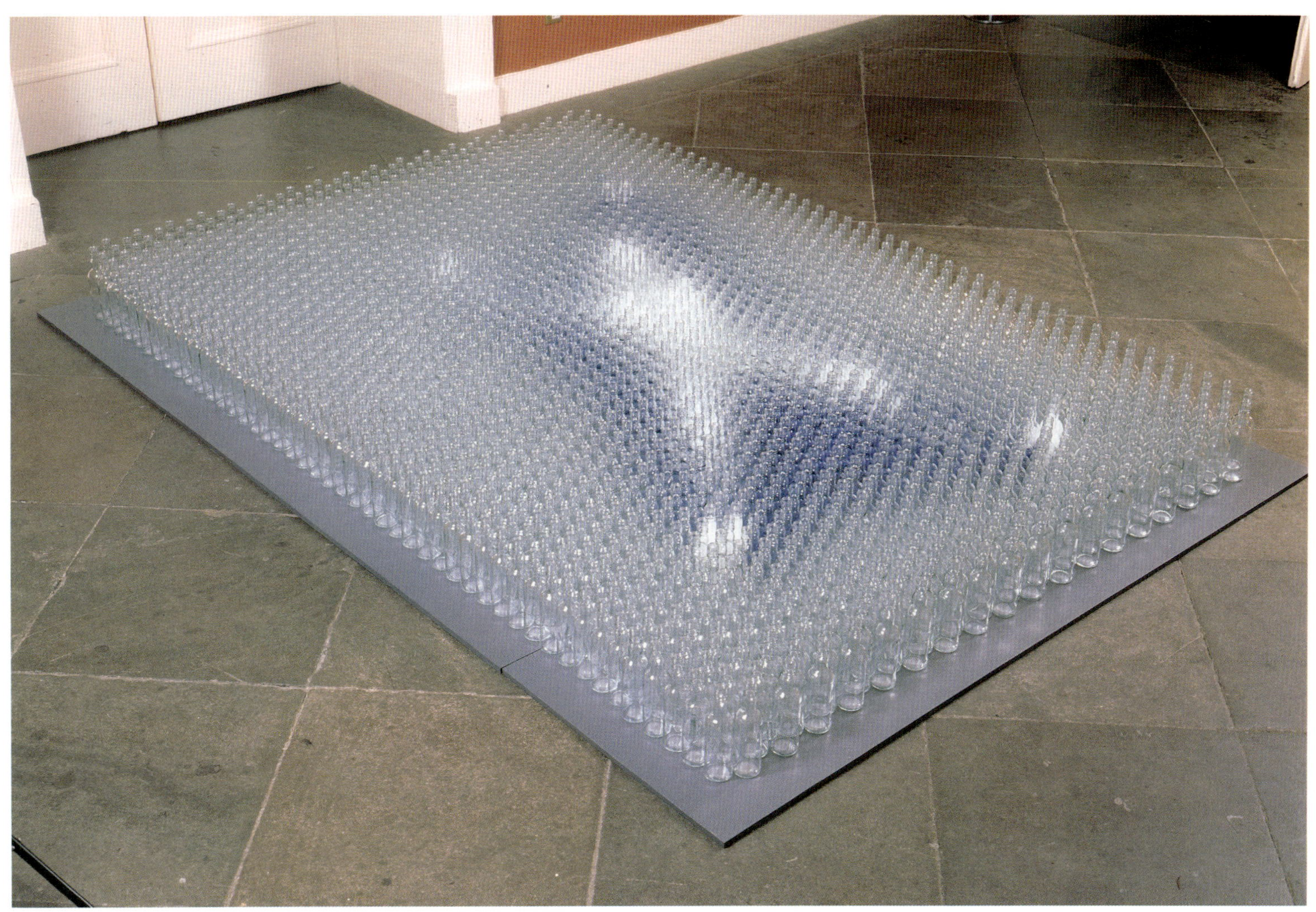

DYING FOR IT / Collection - Scottish National Gallery of Modern Art / June 1989 / Photographer - Colin Reid

Following Page : LIBERTÉ, ÉGALITÉ, FRATERNITÉ - A NEW UTOPIA / Galerie Nikki Diana Marquardt, Paris / June 1989

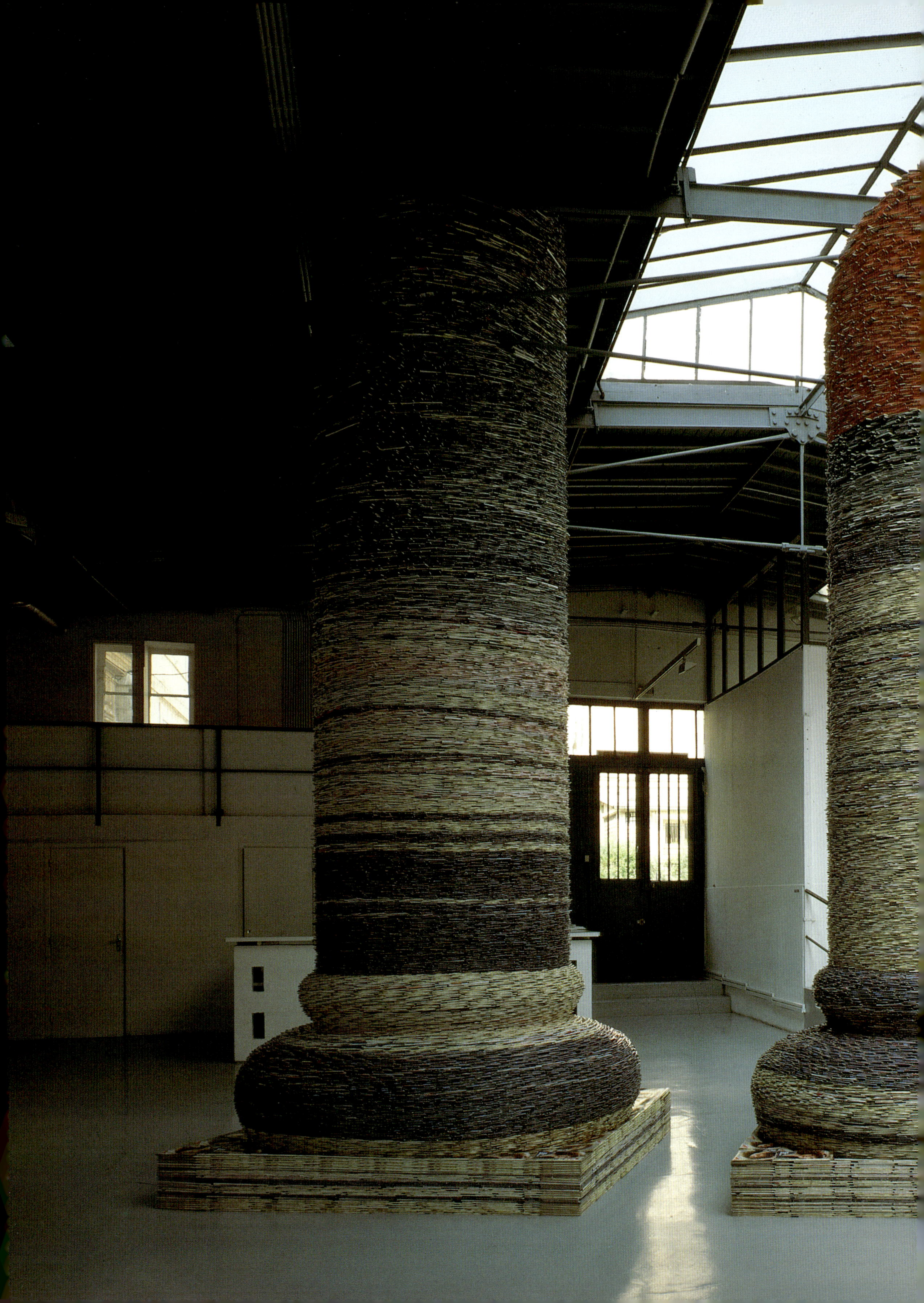

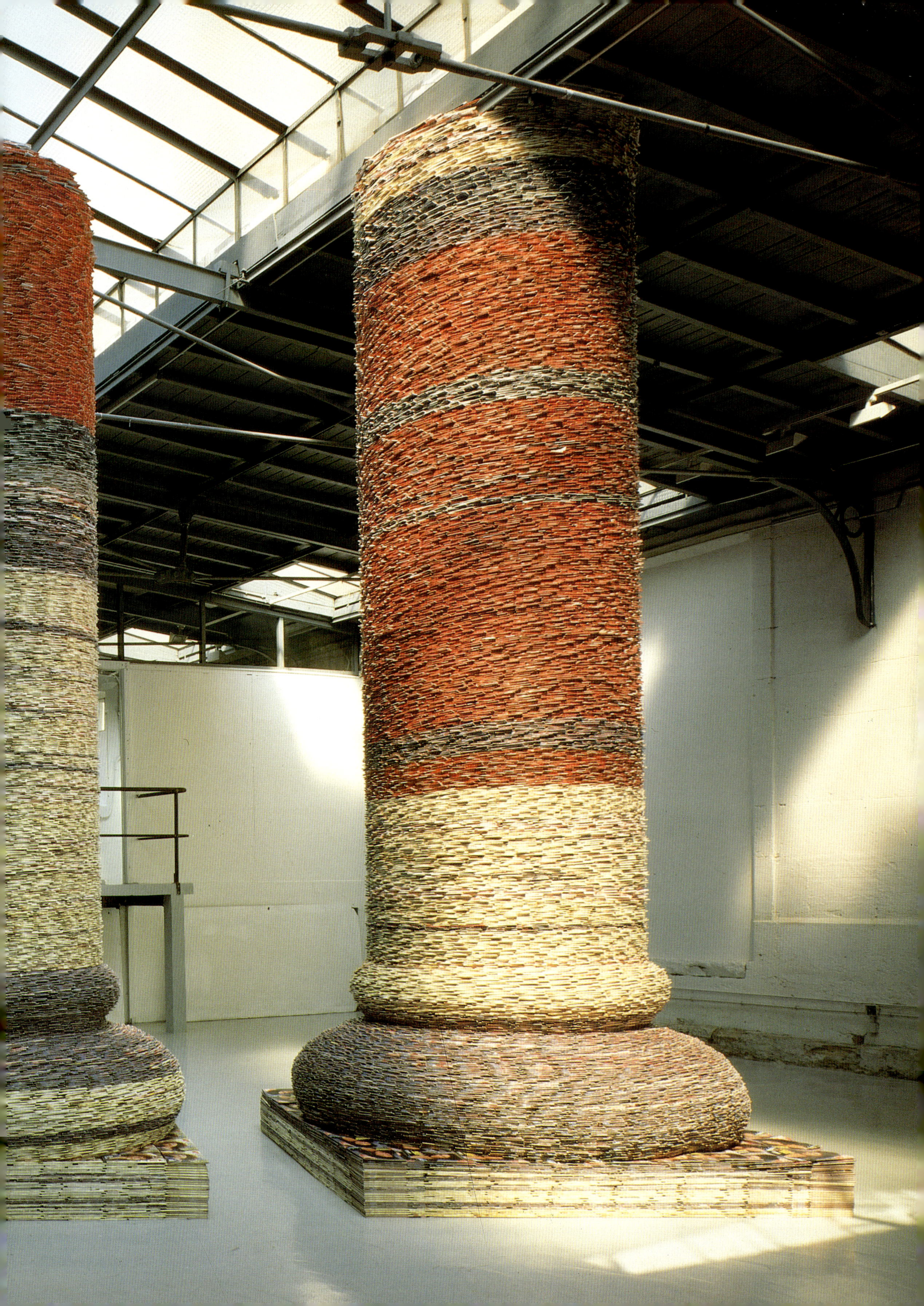

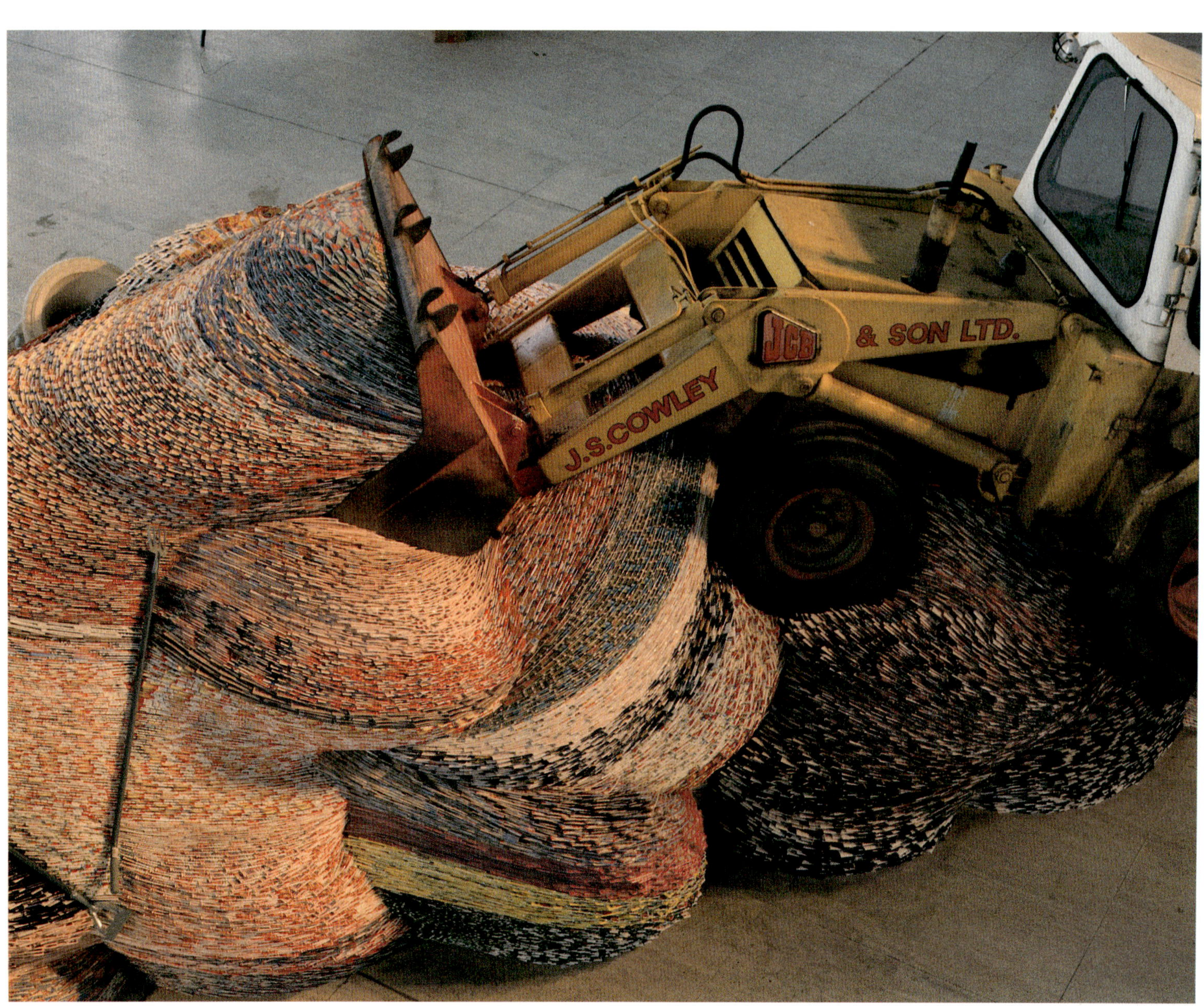

PLOUGHMAN'S LUNCH / Middleton Hall, Milton Keynes / June 1989

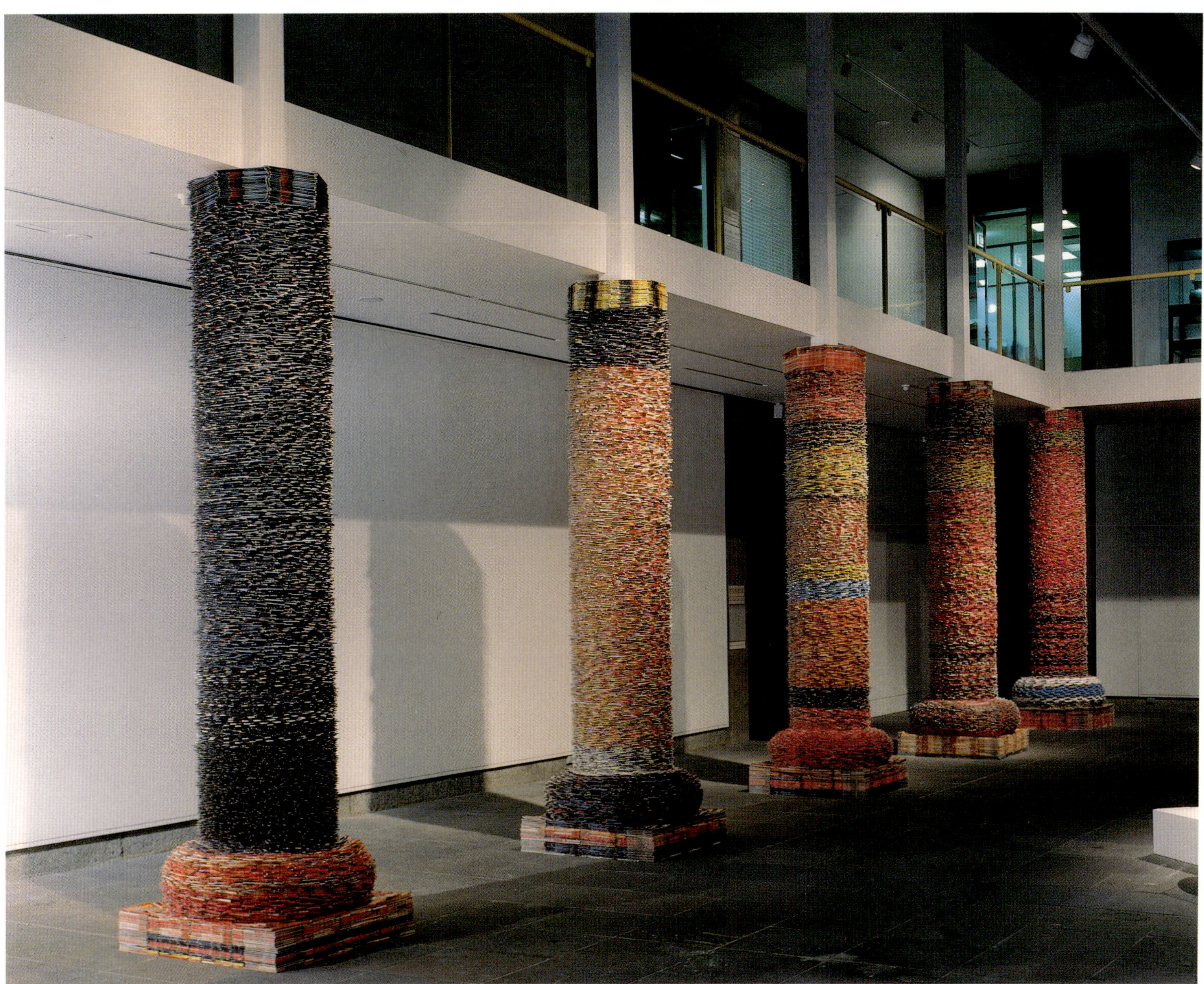

ALONG CLASSICAL LINES / Melbourne Spoleto Festival, National Gallery of Victoria Melbourne
September 1989 / Photographer - Arunas Klupsas

Following Page : WET & DRY / Centro Cultural de la Villa, Madrid / October 1989 / Photographer - Arthur Foster

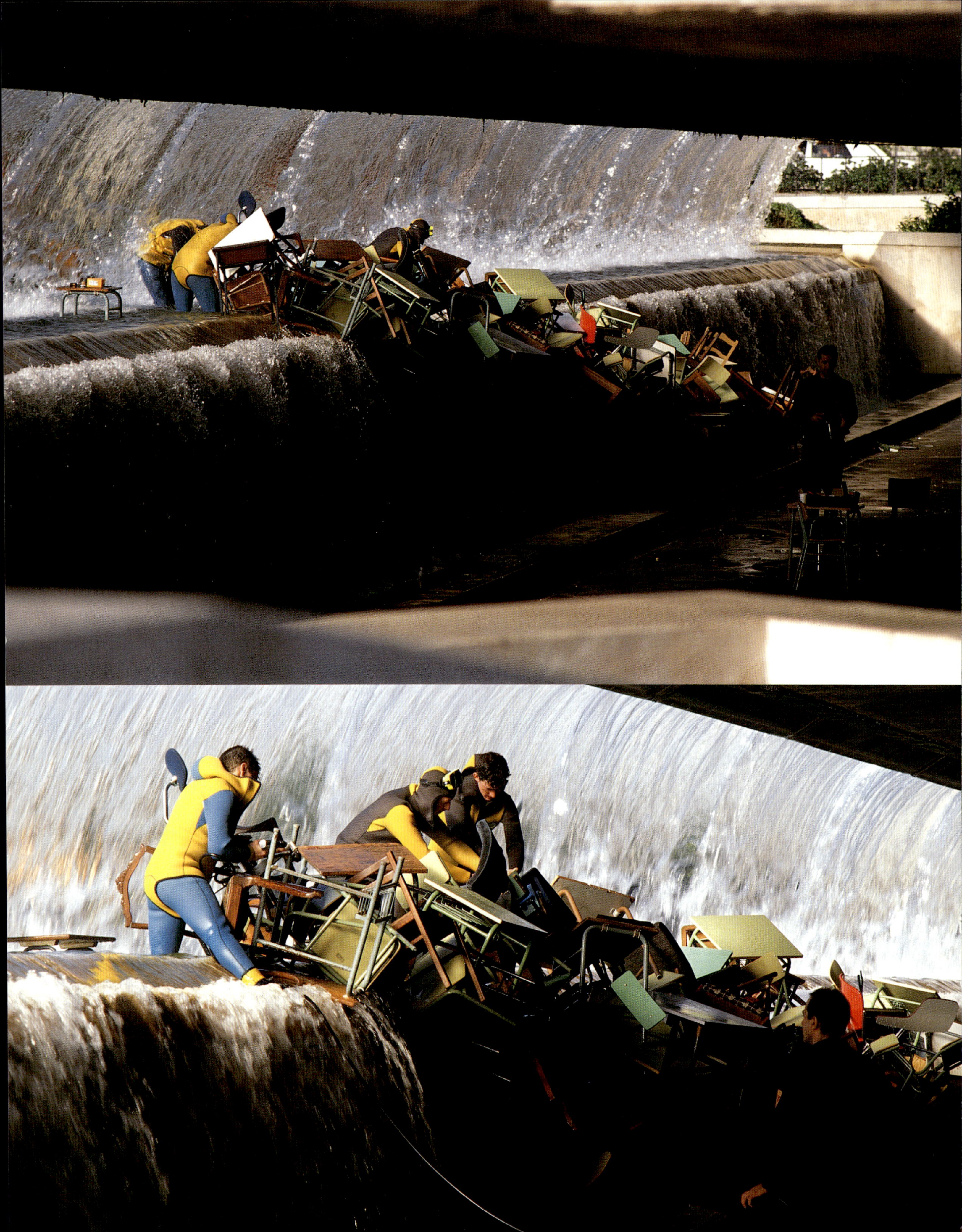